Generation Y in Consumer and Labour Markets

Routledge Interpretive Marketing Research

EDITED BY STEPHEN BROWN, *University of Ulster, Northern Ireland*

Recent years have witnessed an 'interpretive turn' in marketing and consumer research. Methodologies from the humanities are taking their place alongside those drawn from the traditional social sciences.

Qualitative and literary modes of marketing discourse are growing in popularity. Art and aesthetics are increasingly firing the marketing imagination.

This series brings together the most innovative work in the burgeoning interpretive marketing research tradition. It ranges across the methodological spectrum from grounded theory to personal introspection, covers all aspects of the postmodern marketing 'mix', from advertising to product development, and embraces marketing's principal sub-disciplines.

*Also available in Routledge
Interpretive Marketing Research series:*

Generation Y in Consumer and Labour Markets

Anders Parment

Routledge
Taylor & Francis Group

NEW YORK   LONDON

First published 2012
by Routledge
711 Third Avenue, New York, NY 10017

Simultaneously published in the UK
by Routledge
2 Park Square, Milton Park, Abingdon, Oxon OX14 4RN

*Routledge is an imprint of the Taylor & Francis Group,
an informa business*

© 2012 Taylor & Francis

Typeset in Sabon by IBT Global.

Library of Congress Cataloging-in-Publication Data
Parment, Anders, 1972–
   Generation Y in consumer and labour markets / by Anders Parment.
     p. cm. — (Routledge interpretive marketing research ; 15)
   Includes bibliographical references and index.
 1. Generation Y—Economic conditions.   2. Young adult consumers.
3. Generation Y—Employment. I. Title.
   HQ799.5.P37 2011
   331.3'40973—dc22
   2011012949

ISBN13: 978-0-415-88648-2 (hbk)
ISBN13: 978-0-203-80307-3 (ebk)

Contents

Images

FIGURES

PICTURES

Tables

Boxes

Preface

"If young people are not always right, the society that ignores or fights them is always wrong."[1]

There are many newspaper stories, magazine articles, consultant press releases, and an increasing number of books on Generation Y. However, often such reports seem little more than overly generalised and too often Generation Y is presented with a negative bias based on a combination of a lack of understanding about what shaped this generation, and anecdotal examples. Taken together, this results in Generation Y not being presented in a beneficial or adequate way. Well aware of the risk of making such statements I would suggest that there is, in general terms, a negative bias in older people's way of describing younger colleagues, generations, politicians or whatever the younger people's role might be. Ever since Socrates described young people in negative terms—or even earlier—tensions among generations has been an issue:

> Our youth now love luxury. They have bad manners, contempt for authority; they show disrespect for their elders and love chatter in place of exercise; they no longer rise when elders enter the room; they contradict their parents, chatter before company; gobble up their food and tyrannize their teachers.[2]

Lindsey Pollack, American expert on Generation Y, finds it troublesome with the negative attitudes people hold on Generation Y. Pollack is basing her experiences on *research focused exclusively on Millennial women in five countries—the U.S., U.K., Japan, France and Brazil.*

> It's not easy for twentysomething women these days.
> Every day there are stories in the media about Generation Y: They have helicopter parents who run their lives! They are a "lost generation" who will never find jobs! They are coddled and entitled and can't pay attention for more than 140 characters at a time!
> While there are certainly truths underneath these headlines—many Gen Ys look for parental support, they are facing a very tough job market and they love texting—I've often wondered why, particularly in today's challenging times, we aren't eager to seek out more positive

stories about our future leaders. In my experience working with and studying Millennials for the past eight years, I've found a large majority of them to be amazingly optimistic, innovative and courageous—particularly the women, many of whom have grown up with access to more life options than any generation of women in history.[3]

Practitioners alike may have problems with younger people, e.g., this senior project leader in an international sales organisation:

> Generation Yers I got in contact with have a very different approach, and my wife who works for an auditing firm shares this experience. Yers I've been in contact with through jobs and through my wife, who works for an auditing firm, evince some not very nice characteristics: They are egoistic, not very loyal, they want to reach self-realisation, and they are lazy . . . will your book discuss the fact that Yers that will be in the labour market are often academics with a foreigner background? (male, born in 1974)

Many things shape people's—and, in aggregate terms—society's attitudes towards a generation. This book, and largely everything written and said about a generation, makes a significant contribution to the attitudes and myths people perpetuate.

As we will see, there are good reasons to assume that Generation Y will keep up with their predecessors in many of the respects often associated with "youths being non-mature".

This book is an attempt to deal with Generation Y in a more systematic, research-based way. The foundation of the book is two-fold. Firstly, a substantial research body on characteristics and behaviours of the Generation Y, including their relation to other generations and the role of understanding generations in developing effective and attractive organisations. Second, experiences and best practice for reaching, attracting, recruiting, selling to and communicating with Generation Y, based on my experiences from hundreds of organisations where I have worked as a consultant.

This book deals with Generation Y particularly, in both consumer and labour markets. Seldom has there been a study of both. By tradition, political science scholars and economists have studied labour markets, mostly from a structural point of view; marketing scholars have studied consumers; and psychologists and HR scholars have dealt with the individual in the labour market. Over time, there has been an increase in cross-disciplinary and integrative research, and new streams of research have emerged while established research fields have been subject to compartmentalisation.

Hence, this book belongs to inter-disciplinary research and from a theoretical perspective, it is founded on an eclectic tradition that has the empirical phenomenon—Generation Y—in the foreground. Sociology has had a strong impact on the theoretical development during the Generation Y research project that this book deals extensively with. Researchers in management and business are used to dealing with perspectives, theories and models emanating from sociology. The impact of sociology on research in the less mature fields of business, management and marketing have been strong and in some subdisciplines, sociology may even be the most significant theoretical heritage.

Theoretically, the book will contribute to the understanding of generations in marketing research, and the impact of generations (and age) in employee–employer relations.

HOW IT ALL STARTED

As director of studies for business students in years 2005 through 2008 I was in contact with Generation Y on a daily basis. There was something with this group of people that made me confused. On the one hand they were demanding and raised many questions I wasn't used to. On the other hand they were nice and ambitious. Being straightforward and open with their wants was perceived by me as an advantage. They asked me or whoever was in charge instead of complaining and engaging in negative small-talk. As an indication of what had happened in the last 10 to 15 years, there were university course modules that received 3.5 grading when I was a student in the mid-1990s, but we hardly had any comments. One decade later, the same or similar courses got 4.5 and students had many comments—with few exceptions very constructive feedback.

A NOTE ON METHOD

Writing a book certainly is not a trivial endeavour, but in the case of this book, all phases from data collection to writing the conclusions have been characterised by a great deal of pleasure. Writing about generational cohorts is really interesting and there are always new nuances and ideas on how individuals—and generations—could be understood.

The data collection started in Dornbirn, Austria, in Autumn 2006. In 2006 and 2007, 35 interviews with people from Germany, Austria, Sweden, Belgium, Spanien, Mexico, the U.S. and India were conducted. The interviewees represented study subjects such as business administration, economics, law, theology and other social sciences subjects. Some interviewees had no study background at all. Two surveys were sent to students, the first of them referred to as the "Generation Y survey" with 474 respondents (49.4% reply quota). The second one was sent to both the Generation Y and the baby boomer cohorts, the latter cohort also being researched through 20 in-depth interviews. The findings of the baby boomer cohort were presented in a book (Parment, 2008d), which received a prize as Marketing

Book of the Year by the Swedish Marketing Association. Despite of this the baby boomer book has sold less than a tenth compared to the Generation Y book, both published in 2008. The results from the empirical studies on Generation Y have been presented in Parment (2007a, 2007b, 2008c, 2008d, 2009c).

In late 2008 three focus groups with, in total, 20 individuals, were conducted on the theme "Generation Y in the labour market". A new survey was derived from the focus groups with 534 respondents, referred to as the "Employer Branding survey". The results were presented in *Sustainable Employer Branding*, published in April 2009 by Liber/Samfundsforlaget. More focus groups and seminars were held in 2009 and 2010 to substantiate the findings. A multinational survey run together with a group of researchers from the US and New Zealand is running now and data are collected in the U.S., Canada, Brazil, Sweden and New Zealand. Figues 6.2 through 6.4 represent data from the international 2011 survey.

The book has an international appeal and is written to appeal to an international audience. However, it is unavoidable that there will be some bias in the book, since my experiences are limited primarily to Europe, but partly also to America, Australia and Russia. I have recent experiences of writing books with no or few domestic readers. In May 2009, I finished a German book on Generation Y (Gabler Verlag) and it is primarily based on German examples and has a lot of German references. A number of academic journal articles are now in the publishing process, dealing with subjects such as "Generational cohorts in the workplace" and "Seven European generational cohorts". In writing a Scandinavian edition of Kotler and Armstrong's Principles of Marketing, I had to work a lot with the balance between having a general, multinational appeal on the one hand, and emphasising my own experiences, a tricky thing when dealing with the strongly U.S.-biased content of Kotler and Armstrong's original edition.

In writing this book, I was also triggered by the multitude of ideas on Generation Yers—and other cohorts—which were based on research institutes and others that relied on survey studies solely. Researchers have known for ages that surveys certainly might be used for measuring attitudes, behavioural traits and preferences, given the fact that the issue at hand is clearly defined and the context of the issue is understood. However, in many cases, using surveys solely is a dangerous practice. There is a substantial risk the context and fundamental mechanisms of the behaviour one wants to understand are not understood. There are many instances of this, e.g., that of an internationally operating research company specialised in defining and understanding generations—in 2007 they suggested that people born in the 1990s are characterised by "Indian values", meaning they will work heavily to realise their life intentions (very unlikely in the context of the Nordic countries!). In 2010, however, the same company suggested that people born in the 1990s want a calm family wife, and many females want to be housewives for a lifetime. Two insights come to me: First, attitudes change fast during the coming-of-age years, and people born in the 1990s are still there. One explanation might be that too many of them get inspired by the *Desperate Housewives* and similar influences in the popular cultural sphere. Second, surveys must be part of a broader data collection and understanding of the phenomena at hand.

Apart from the limitations that my country of origin result in, I realise that my perspective is restricted also in some other respects, and that may limit the applicability of the findings presented in this book. I'm born in September 1972 and I lived most of my life in Sweden. I'm a male and lived most of my life in city and metro areas. So my experiences are certainly restricted when it comes to understanding baby boomers, females, Italy and remote areas with hardly anybody living there. I have a high level of education but that not only makes me see things, it may also restrict my perspectives. My father is a retired political scientist and he often says I'm too focused on successful people when I'm writing. Sure, I'm a marketer and I'm more interested in people who buy than those who don't. My brother sometimes criticises me for similar reasons. So my perspective is certainly limited. My parents brought me to many interesting places in the world at an early stage in my life, and my fantastic family and many great friends gave—and give—me perspectives and ideas. I think I have a diversified group of people around me in my social setting, but it's probably less diversified than I believe—just like CEOs use to say "I want no yes-men" but nonetheless they recruit people like themselves to the board of directors.

There is a lot of frustration out there and it's often linked to individuals' aging and gender issues. Not only interviews but also everyday conversations have expanded, and certainly in some senses restricted, my horizon. One is always—in the social sciences particularly—under influence from everyday conversations, which is basically a good thing and a key source of observations and ideas. An Austrian baby boomer colleague was chocked when I told him I'll be on paternity leave for six months: "Who is going to do the job?" He's the kind of guy who is involved in everything and hardly shows up at home until 10 at night. And some Swedish baby boomer colleagues show frustration when they understand what is going on—a shift of generations that means they reach the end of their careers and become replaced by individuals often younger than their own children. All types of arguments have been provided, e.g., as put by a baby boomer professor: "the young professors in our board have too little experience" (they are 43 and 48 . . .), "I'm born in the 1950s and for the first time I realise that I'm exactly as you describe Generation Y" (after listening to his 10-minute monologue about his life frustrations and the problems of today's youth, he was obviously wrong).

I met a German couple in their early 40s at a wedding. The man, an engineer and middle manager in a multinational corporation, really wanted to be on paternity leave, and his behaviour during the wedding suggested he meant what he said. However, as he said, "I certainly can tell my employer that I will be on leave for six months, and he has to accept it, but he would start making life very difficult for me". Not only laws and policies but also employer attitudes matter. Fortunately, his wife's profession was M.D., and she said "My employer doesn't give me an establishment so I have to work on short term contracts. But as a MD I know I'll always get new contracts. There is a lot of jobs and contracts out there for a skilled doctor." This couple was lucky to have the opportunity to stay at home with their children *and* make a good career—something very difficult in many countries. Two interesting things became very obvious to me when I talked to this couple. First, like many younger individuals, they understood the power of market mechanisms—if one is attractive in the labour market, one doesn't need to follow the employer's ideas on whether one can be on mother's leave, take a month off and travel through Asia, or work the entire summer and have no vacation until the late autumn. Qualified coworkers are in power and Generation Y particularly is aware of this. Second, in countries with little financial and institutional help from the state for maternity and paternity leave (i.e., most countries, with Scandinavia as an exception), there is a high risk that the development towards equality among the sexes slows down. In Austria I was sad to hear that young females had the choice of either making a career or staying at home with the children which, in combination with the built-in effects of the Austrian education system (it's hard to catch up if one has chosen the wrong track during primary and secondary school), makes it hard to believe in an emerging equality among the sexes in years to come. And, again, the popular culture has an influence: *Desperate Housewives* and other similar television programmes may influence young females to maintain old gender structures.

Along the way, I met many people who contributed to strengthening my skills in analyzing generations. Many people deserve to be mentioned here, but from my research perspective, the person that has been most important in developing my skills is Charles Schwede, professor in Marketing at the Isenberg School of Management, University of Massachusetts. Charles who was one of the first to develop cohorts marketing, not only gave me inspiration and an extended framework, he also contributed with his 30 years of experience from research in the field.

Needless to say, I'm responsible for any mistakes or misinterpretations along the way of writing this book.

Stockholm, May 2011
Anders Parment

1 Introduction

This book deals with Generation Y, people born in the 1980s, or in the late 1970s, and their role in consumer and labour markets. Young consumers, and to a certain extent Generation Y, have been subject to a great deal of research from a marketing perspective. However, in labour markets this emerging generation will also have a strong impact by bringing a new set of ideas, values and attitudes to the employee–employer relationship and how work is being done. Employers are increasingly asked by employees to offer a nice work environment, attractive terms and personal development, thus reflecting Generation Y's need for self-realisation at work—ideals that may be derived from Generation Y's coming-of-age in our consumption-oriented society. On the one hand, the changes cause frustration and generational conflicts. On the other hand, organisations need a demanding, creative and flexible workforce to stay competitive in a world of fierce competition, cost pressure and increasingly demanding customers.

Generation Y individuals have grown up in a branded society over-crowded with commercial messages and a never-ending supply of choices and opportunities. On consumer markets, they are demanding, aware of their rights and loyalty is limited in general terms. They see brands as an integrated part of consumption and personal image-building. Thus, personal branding (Dr. Phil, Karl Lagerfeld, Madonna and many other celebrities), employer branding (Apple, Google and IKEA) and place branding (Barcelona, Birmingham and Sydney) are something natural. Virtual networking, new communication technologies and intensive feedback are natural parts of everyday life. These changes and tendencies cannot be explained by the age of Generation Y individuals alone. A number of changes at different levels—society, the market environment, the social environment, and the way organisations respond to the emerging situation—taken together create a new situation for individuals who behave differently than earlier generations at the same age. As a consequence, individuals' attitudes, priorities and choices—essentially their behaviour as consumers and coworkers—will change.

Given the attention paid to environmental scanning, market intelligence and different facets of the macro environment in marketing research and literature, the concept of generation has not been elaborated sufficiently. The concept of generations is inherently different from the concept of age, although both may give similar results and recommendations in some applications. The ambition of the book is to reach across age and generational boundaries to understand Generation Y. Thus, with Generation Y in focus, the book will introduce the concept of generations and generational analysis as an important concept in understanding markets and the behaviour of individuals as consumers and coworkers. The analysis covers four levels of analysis, thus mirroring the dialectics between society, the market environment, the social environment and how people think and behave as individuals and coworkers. The analytical framework lays the foundation for the analysis of Generation Y in the book, but may be used also for analysing other generations.

The book will present a challenging outcome of this emerging society: Consumer and labour markets converge in some critical dimensions. Generation Y sees work as a venue of self-realisation and the boundaries between work and leisure time are becoming blurred in an emerging postmodernist society with a multitude of choices and lifestyles, high transparency in many dimensions and strong market forces, which reduce the influence by the state.

This book is based on an assumption that to understand consumer and employee behaviour, one needs to understand both the environment and the individual, thus integrating insights from marketing and environmental scanning with consumer behaviour analysis. Companies try to link opportunities in the environment to market potential in selling to consumers and, from the perspective of this book, coworkers are often crucial in this process as bearers and communicators of the company's values and culture.

The aim of this book is twofold. Firstly, to discuss the emergence of Generation Y in consumer and labour markets. Second, to gain deeper insights into the interplay between different elements of society in understanding generations, i.e., to substantiate and develop the model of four levels that are assumed to shape a generation (society, market environment, social environment and individuals). Thus, in a sense, the book will bring together two different streams of research by extending the analysis of how Generation Y acts in consumer markets to an analysis of how the Generation Y cohort relates to work and career.

THE STUDY OF GENERATIONS

Studies of generations already exist in a number of research fields, and they have an identifiable place within the field of sociology particularly, where Karl Mannheim's *Problem of Generations* (1960) lays the foundation of research in sociology on this matter. Particularly useful to the exploration of generations is Mannheim's distinction between generational location, i.e., individuals born in the same historical and cultural region such as *birth cohort*, or actual generation, i.e., individuals exposed to the same historical experiences (cf. the discussion on defining moments in this and the next chapter), and *generational units*, i.e., interpreting similar experiences in different ways depending on which generation the person belongs to.

Karl Mannheim's work challenges the boundaries of Generation Y, including social bonds, into biological understandings of age and generational cohorts. Individuals within the same historical time period may have different interpretations of what happened during the period. Mannheim emphasises that interactions formed within or across generations may represent *cultural exchange*.

Mannheim also deals with the process by which the cultural transmission between generations takes place. During periods of rapid social change, strains towards discontinuity between generations are intensified. Mannheim suggests that *"The rate of social change increases the likelihood that new generations will break from the tradition"* (Mannheim, 1952, pp. 309–310). Thus, a turbulent societal environment is likely to result in more pronounced differences between generations.

The suggestion made in this book is that the study of generations has been underemphasised in the fields of business and management. Thus, the perspective taken is strongly influenced by the emphasis on generations in studies carried out by sociologists. Companies are likely to benefit from understanding the generation dimension in their striving for competitiveness and organisational effectiveness.

Elder (1994) in one of the most quoted articles on sociology, emphasises the strong influence of generations in the social sciences, and how it emerged during the 1960s to 1980s. Elder starts by referring to the situation around 1960:

> The concept of life course, however, as we know it today (Elder 1992a, but see Cain 1964), was not to be found in the scholarly literature. It did not appear in sociological or psychological theory or in the coursework of our leading graduate programs. I left graduate studies without any exposure to, or understanding of, the life course as field of inquiry, theory, or method. Today we find that life course thinking has diffused across disciplinary boundaries and specialty areas within particular disciplines (Featherman, 1983). Application of the perspective in sociology extends across the subfields of population, social stratification, complex organisations, family, criminology, and medical sociology, among other. Beyond sociology, life course studies appear in social history (Elder, Modell, and Parke 1993; Modell 1989), developmental psychology (Bronfenbrenner 1979), and gerontology. . . . (Elder, 1994, p. 4)

It appears to be a remarkable lack of interest for generations in business and management research in general. Grenier (2007) argues that while

gender, race/ethnicity and class are clearly articulated in the research literature (see, e.g., Oakley, 1981; Phoenix, 1994), age and generation remain
undertheorised fields. Hence, as this book will show, marketing as a field of
study is also in great need of the generational dimension. Consumer behaviour research focuses on age and behavioural traits of children, teenagers
and other age cohorts (see, e.g., Evans et al., 2009), but hardly discusses
this in generational terms.

The literature on two generations specifically—Generation Y and baby
boomers—has expanded in recent years. The majority of the literature on
Generation Y focuses on their attitudes towards established norms and
societal institutions (Huntley, 2006; Martin & Tulgan, 2001; Tulgan,
2009); their traits at work (Chester, 2002; Lipkin & Perrymore, 2009;
Martin & Tulgan, 2001; Tulgan, 2009); and how to deal with conflicts
between generations (Gravett & Throckmorton, 2007). To an extent, this
stream of literature is based on research, but there is a lack of integration
with marketing thinking, and the lack of theorising makes these research
results more geared towards practitioners. Few books deal with baby
boomers in the workplace—if baby boomers at work are treated, it is
in the context of conflicts between generations, etc. (Gravett & Throckmorton, 2007). As baby boomers are in the last years of their careers,
but have in aggregate terms high purchase power and more time than
younger consumers (Gerstner & Hunke, 2006; Parment, 2008d), there is
reason to expect the interest in baby boomers as consumers to be higher.
There are numerous books on this subject area, at least 25 in English and
13 in German (as a contrast, there is only one book on Generation Y in
German). A few of these books are based on substantial research, e.g.,
Ian Chaston's *Boomer Marketing. Selling to a Recession Resistant Market* (2009) and to an extent Brent Green's *Marketing to Leading Edge
Baby Boomers* (2003).

In research journals there are a few articles on marketing to generations, e.g., Herbig, Koehler, and Day (1993) on what they call the *baby
bust generation*—a concept hardly used recently—that is, children of the
baby boomers. Roberts and Manolis (2000) compare baby boomers and
baby busters in few consumer behaviour dimensions. Bakewell and Mitchell (2003) study the decision making of adult female Generation Y consumers. Littrell, Yoon, and Halepete (2005) compare the attitudes towards
fair trade among Generation X (age 29–40) and Swing (age 65–70).

To an extent, marketing scholars have been applying life course theory, e.g., for the study of brand loyalty (cf. Higgs et al., 2009; White &
Klein, 2007). All in all, there appears to be a lack of recent studies that
help us understand generational cohorts and their overall implications for
consumer and labour markets. And as most available studies are rather
restricted in their approach, we need to go beyond relatively limited studies
of a few aspects of what constitutes a generation to get a broader picture of
what Generation Y means to society, businesses and individuals.

GENERATIONS AND AGE

Age cohorts should not be confused with the very meaning of generations. The former does not really consider the societal conditions, while the latter emphasises that different periods may imply different values, societal priorities and critical collective experiences, e.g., the Cold War, the 9/11 terror attacks, the emergence of the Internet and the behavioural traits that came with it, political change, and the economic climate. It has been suggested that Generation Y grew up with a fundamentally different set of values, since there was unbroken economic growth and the end of the Cold War changed the attitudes towards fear and wars (cf. Meredith & Schewe, 1994; Schewe & Meredith, 2004).

With a generational perspective, people are expected to relate to environmental considerations and the climate discussion in different ways depending on how society overall deals with these issues. Thus, research results on the attitude towards ecological and environmentally friendly food among people aged 20 to 29 may vary vastly depending on which year data were collected. Twenty-year-old data on the matter means that another generation answered the questions in another societal setting (environmental concerns were less heavy at the time), so although they were 20 to 29 when data were collected the findings cannot be used without thought-through reinterpretation.

While age has for a long time been used as a segmentation variable, generations have not been discussed in this context until quite recently. Age being an established concept in marketing, few would disagree with Eisenstadt's (1956) comment that "Age and differences of age are among the most basic and crucial aspects of human life and determinants of human destiny" (p. 21). However, there are strong reasons to complement the concept of age with that of generations, and integrate research from other disciplines, e.g., sociology.

Sociologists generally recognise that age groups are a product of the interaction of biological and social factors, and the phenomenon of generations is seen as the biological rhythm of birth and death (Mannheim, 1952; O'Donnell, 1985). According to O'Donnell (1985), a generation in its broadest usage comprises all those members of a society *"who were born approximately at the same time, whether or not they are related by blood"* (p. 2). Mannheim (1956) distinguishes between location, to be located or coexist with others of the same age, and generation as actuality, meaning individuals who share a community of experience and feeling.

The major body of research on age and generations has been done decades ago and to a large extent it has been done by sociologists. The majority of sociologists studying the concept of generations emphasise the dialectics between individuals and their behaviour, and social structure (cf. White Riley, 1982), thus mirroring society as the primary unit of analysis. Moreover, sociologists suggest that generation and age are different principles, the former having meaning in family and the latter in society as a whole

(Kertzer, 1983). However, this varies with country and culture, and the muddling of the distinction between generation and age cohort causes confusion. According to Fry & Keith (1982), the number of age grades, the centrality of reproductive careers in determining life course stage, and the use of chronological age to allocate social positions vary within and between societies.

At least in Western societies, Internationalisation and Globalisation have fundamentally changed the patterns of life cycles, at least from a consumption perspective, and made them less restricted by country and culture (cf. Alden, 1999). In every country a multitude of consumption cultures emerge, and they may be shared by a particular generation, geographic location, political interest or professional association. With our ambition to explore the generational cohort dimension, it is crucial to keep in mind that other factors than generational belonging may be crucial in understanding the situation at hand.

THE COMING-OF-AGE EXPERIENCES AS FOUNDATION OF THE ANALYSIS OF GENERATIONS

The book rests on two assumptions. First, the assumption that individuals' values and preferences are shaped by a broad set of values and forces at (i) a *societal level* (e.g., collectivism versus individualism, modernistic values that favour industrialism, rationalism and functionalism as opposed to postmodernistic values); (ii) the *market environment* that reflects supply and demand mechanisms and the availability of products from the global marketplace; and (iii) the *social environment* that represents how people relate to each other under influence from contemporary popular culture and the technology available.

Second, the assumption that coming-of-age experiences influence values, attitudes, behaviour, and how individuals relate to consumer and labour markets for a lifetime. A substantial body of research suggests that individuals are highly influenced by the external events that were happening when they were coming of age (generally between the years 17 to 23, but also to an extent in years before 17). The Great Depression, the Cold War, Watergate, the energy crisis in the 1970s, 9/11, the Assassination of Olof Palme, the reunion of Western and Eastern Germany and the end of the Franco era in Spain are examples of major events that distinguish one age cohort from another. Some events are global by nature, e.g., the Cold War, and some others are local, e.g., the end of the Franco era, but all events may have a varying impact across geographical areas, cultures, generations and individuals depending on their character.

In the social sciences in general, and in marketing in particular, one dimension can hardly constitute the only prediction of behaviour, nor can it be seen as the overriding explanatory factor. There are, in most cases, too many intertwined factors in a complex set of explanatory and response variables, driving forces and effects so the result of the analysis will ultimately depend upon the perspective chosen and assumptions made. This book assumes generations to be important in understanding decisions and policy making in companies' actions in consumer and labour markets. The message of the book is not necessarily that the concept of generations is more important than other factors in understanding consumer behaviour and developing marketing strategies. However, at the same time, the book rests on a conviction that generations must be taken into consideration in developing viable and successful strategies.

AGE AND GENERATIONAL COHORT—
THE DANGER OF MIXING THEM UP

Table 1.1 shows a typical demographic profile of the drinks market. There are significant differences in terms of how different age groups consume beer, wine and whisky. The key question with the perspective taken in this book is: Will individuals stay more or less with the same consumption patterns as they get older (indicating that generational cohort explains spending) or will they drink more whisky and less beer and wine when they get older (indicating that age explains spending)?

Table 1.1 Typical Demographic Profile of the Drinks Market. From Evans, Jamal, & Foxall (2006)

	Beer (%)	*Wine (%)*	*Whisky (%)*
Age			
18–24	58	23	7
25–34	50	29	8
35–49	45	28	14
50+	30	15	17
Social Grade			
AB	39	40	17
C1	40	30	14
C2	48	20	13
D, E	38	9	10
Gender			
Male	65	22	19
Female	21	22	8

As this example shows, age defined as chronological age (i.e., date of birth) and generational cohorts diverge over time. A journal article from 1991 may be based on data from 1988—thus reflecting a time when younger baby boomers were as young as individuals in the Generation Y cohort are now. Considering the fact that these groups are sometimes contrasted with baby boomers, the relation between age and when data were collected appears to be crucial. In the worst case, one tries to gain information about some aspects of how Generation Y would behave in a typical situation, but gets information about baby boomers. The results may nonetheless be applicable to many marketing and management situations, but one needs to be aware about the inherent differences between age and generation. To give another example, Cockrell, Cockrell, and Harris (1998) study the understanding and use of technology among students *"aged 20–27, representing the mid-range of the Generation-X-cohort, examined their technological attitudes, knowledge, and usage in comparison to those of the Baby Boom cohort"* (p. 111). Had it not been for the explicitness on generational belonging, one could mistakenly have thought that the data would be directly applicable to Generation Y—more than a decade later, attitudes towards technology at a particular age are likely to have shifted.

MARKETING AND HR PERSPECTIVES

This book takes marketing rather than HR (Human Resources) as the point of departure in framing in the subject area. Thus, the market environment is seen as an important driving force in the development of Generation Y attitudes and behaviour, also in relation to the labour market. The perspective taken is also highly influenced by sociologists, an interest to an extent shared by business, management, marketing and consumer behaviour researchers. With this perspective taken, the book may be useful for marketers, HR managers and others who deal with Generation Y and generational conflicts.

In recent years, the HR department has taken on a more strategic role in the organisation, and HR managers have been moving from a traditional caring perspective, to a more strategic perspective. This development mirrors an increasing importance of recruiting the right employees to stay competitive (Barrow & Mosley, 2005; Parment & Dyhre, 2009).

Developing strategies to appeal to Generation Y will be crucial for many organisations in preparing for the future. For instance, working more systematically with attracting and recruiting employees that share the values and sympathise with the policies and work method approaches applied by the company creates a more consistent and sound organisation, both in terms of its way of functioning (smooth and effective) and in attracting and recruiting further employees. Important to note, this does not mean coworkers should be a homogenous group of individuals who agree on everything. Diversity is crucial in terms of coworkers' age, sex, background, family set-up and social setting. A diversified workforce provides more perspectives and ideas, it is less exposed to specific risks (e.g., a homogenous group of coworkers who quit at short notice as a protest activity; 63-year-old coworkers who lose energy and plan for retirement; parents of children during flu times, etc.) and there is less tendency a negative jargon develops. The latter may irritate new employees—or employees who deviate from the dominant culture and jargon—and make them less attracted by what the employee offers. All in all, a diversified workforce with coworkers who largely share the view on customers and how work should be done, etc., facilitates the work efforts and makes the organisation a more attractive employer.

Most organisations need to work with Employer Branding in a systematic, thought-through way to be attractive—and communicate their attractiveness—in relation to Generation Y and also other young professionals who see work as a venue of self-realisation. This is a great opportunity for different departments in the organisation—particularly HR and marketing—to start cooperating. Typically, the HR department and the marketing department find their roles very different, and sometimes people in these departments may even be suspicious about each other: The marketing department puts pressure on the organisation by pushing the expectations too high, while the HR department has more of a caring and reactive role (cf. Parment & Dyhre, 2009). This has been approved in studies, e.g., one conducted by SHL who make and interpret psychometric tests. Their 1990s test of psychometrics of HR executives, which may still be useful, compared with those of other management disciplines provides the following results:

Table 1.2 Psychometric Characteristics of HR People Compared to Other Management Disciplines (From Barrow & Mosley, 2007)

HR people are more	*HR people are less*
Affiliative	Persuasive
Democratic	Data rational
Caring	Innovative
Behavioural	Organised and structured
Worrying	Critical
	Competitive

THE ROLE OF GENERATIONAL COHORTS IN MARKETING

The marketing discipline attempts to identify and use consumer characteristics in order to be better prepared to market and sell products in a way that appeals to the desired consumers—addressed as individuals or segments depending on the marketing situation at hand. Hence, effectiveness is crucial in approaching consumers: From time to time and situation to situation, various dimensions and variables may appear to be particularly important. For instance, gender balance has been found to be important in creating effective sales organisations (Moncrief, Babakus, Cravens, & Johnston, 2000); differences between metropolitan and rural areas are crucial in reaching car buyers (Parment, 2009a); and a consumer culture perspective that emphasises the role of gender and sex has been found to be crucial in developing promotion and market communication that appeals to younger consumers particularly (Reichert & Lambiase, 2005). Having said this, the very effect of emphasising generations is that the marketer gets one more tool in her toolbox for designing marketing strategies.

THE ROLE OF GENERATIONAL COHORTS AT WORK

The labour market and the conditions for carrying out work effectively and efficiently are ever-changing. Employers are experiencing challenges in recruiting employees, dealing with managing effective teams, and tempering the demands among stakeholders and customer segments. Additionally, customers are now approaching companies differently than in the past. They rely on grassroots and other information disseminated through the Internet in gaining information on the employer, and represent a more questioning attitude towards the employer's employment offer (just like they do in their role as customers with consumer offers and customer policies). However, with a great employer brand the company can remain in power. Although coworkers have always been crucial in developing a strong brand, the coworker must now be involved in a more systematic and profound way in developing the company's competitiveness. This emerging perspective is linked to an increased emphasis on Employer Branding.

As a lot of the literature on Generation Y focuses on highly skilled and talented individuals, it's important to emphasise that Employer Branding in recent years has developed towards a *right talent approach* rather than a *top talent approach*. The following statement is highly relevant:

> The difference between a good and a great company is usually the talent level. (Overholt, 2002)

However, it is important to distinguish between top talents in general terms and top talents in relation to the organisation's mission, strategy and needs for skills and competences. A talent level and profile more adapted to what the employer needs is referred to as a right talent approach. What is a right talent varies by context and situation. In the public sector, the skill to follow principles of public organisations, e.g., treating everybody equally and at the same time be customer-oriented and good at explaining tricky trade-offs between what the public services include and what the citizen wants may be critical. A salesman should not only be good at selling, but also understand the principles of value-based pricing, build long-term customer relations, use her knowledge to provide feedback from customers to the company, and have good relations to product development, conceptual development and engineers. Modern, complex, customised products are not easy to sell, and salesmen don't always understand the engineering side which causes a lot of frustration between parts of the organisation. On the other side there may be engineers, HR departments and architects lacking the market orientation that is necessary to satisfy demands on profitability and customer satisfaction. Top talents with good grades from top universities but the wrong attitude, lack of customer orientation and difficulties in making trade-offs between different interests and demands may find it increasingly difficult to make consistent career progress. On the other hand, people lacking formal qualifications but with great abilities to cooperate, understand customers and combine existing knowledge to find new solutions are likely to make a great contribution to the organisation (cf. Parment & Dyhre, 2009).

The labour market—in aggregate terms—is subject to a profound transition and reorientation. As suggested by Woolridge (2006), talent will be a scarce resource in the future. Woolridge emphasises a number of interesting trends. Intangible assets in the U.S. have shot up from 20% of company values among the S & P 500 companies in 1980 to about 70% in year 2006. The number of tactical jobs, which is the most qualified type in a categorisation made by McKinsey, has increased 2.5 to 3 times as fast as less qualified jobs. At the same time, changing demographics make it increasingly difficult to find the talents organisations need. The ongoing changes are shifting the balance of power from organisations to the workforce, and this development is linked to the attitudinal changes that Generation Y entails will be a challenge for employers in years to come.

The transition of work life has many facets and is driven both by employers, who act under increasing demands on competitiveness, effectiveness and expectations of being socially and environmentally responsible, and employees. The changes on the employee side have been going on for a long time, and there is always an element of change that comes with each new generation of workforce. However, with the entrance of the Generation Y in labour markets, the transition to a new situation is more clearly articulated.

WHY CONSUMER AND LABOUR MARKETS?

Not only in the minds of researchers, but also in most people's understanding, there has been a strong division between the consumption sphere and working life. Modernistic societies, which will be discussed in Chapter 3, emerged and grew under a strong influence from values of reason rather than emotions. Leisure time was seen as a necessary break to charge the batteries physically and mentally, thus making the employee (coworker, which suggests some reciprocity between the organisation and the employee, was not an adequate term at the time) prepared to come back to work as a highly productive individual.

Over time, the division between work and leisure time has become blurred, the state has lost much of its influence on individuals, many authorities have lost their power and values of self-realisation together with an extensive youth period have contributed to attitudinal transitions among people. For Generation Y, who grew up with commercial television, high economic standards and few or no memories of the Cold War and financial crises, it should come as little surprise that the set of values that form the attitudes of this generation are fundamentally different from generations before. From a labour market perspective, this means that organisations need to recruit talented people who fit the values, culture and image of their employer (Barrow & Mosley, 2005; Parment & Dyhre, 2009).

When Generation Y individuals were first interviewed on their attitudes towards consumption (Parment, 2007a), it soon appeared that working life shares many of the inherent characteristics of the consumption sphere. Thus, immaterial values, e.g., the social environment, fun at work and the opportunity to learn and earn merit are seen as the three most important factors in the choice of employer (Parment, 2009c). Even an economic downturn, as in 2008, is not likely to change the general attitudes and priorities of this generation, although it may be more difficult to reach self-realisation at work in the early career for those who graduate and are lucky to start working during the downturn. When it is difficult for a new grad to get a job, the expectations of fun at work and similar priorities may be lower. In fact, it would be difficult to describe the characteristics and understand the behaviour of Generation Y without taking both spheres of consumption and work respectively into consideration, since work and consumption overlap and are both very important parts of everyday life to Generation Y.

Hence, this book takes on a consumer *and* labour market perspective in dealing with Generation Y. This is obviously an odd combination—books used to apply either a consumer *or* a labour market perspective. However, as we will see, for Generation Y, spheres that were earlier dichotomised, at least in analyses and theoretical models, are now to be approached simultaneously from more than one stance. Working and leisure time are increasingly overlapping in terms of content, and they are also converging in Generation Y individuals' preferences on what they expect from life. Old dichotomies are gradually losing their power. Working 9 to 5, having the weekend off and not enjoying a nice dinner until it's Friday are all behavioural traits derived from values that were long established in society. In the emerging society that Generation Y is shaping, these values will still have some power, but less than before, which gives companies that take this transition as an opportunity an advantage.

DEMATERIALISATION OF SOCIETY

An important reason to study consumer and labour markets at the same time is the dematerialisation of society and the changes it entails. In a speech at Harvard University in 1943, Winston Churchill suggested that *"the empires of the future will be empires of the mind"*[1]. This was a great forecast of the development in decades to come. To an increasing extent, talent, values, culture, brands and other immaterial factors play a key role in creating competitiveness. In the old days, workers moved to get a job, but now, companies now may have to move to where the creative people are, which reflects a transition in the power balance between employers and employees.

> Talented people need organisations less than organisations need talented people.[2]

Szita (2007) discusses the creative class—people working with science, technology and marketing—which constitutes about 30% of the workforce in the U.S., compared to 5% in the 1950s. This development, however, does not imply that there is a decreasing need for traditional, material resources. A more reasonable explanation is that there is still heavy competition between nations, philosophies and methods in terms of which material to use in products, choice of fuel in vehicles, trade-off between blue-collar workers and machines, etc. Competition is becoming increasingly global, and apparently, the development of information and communication technologies has made the world more transparent. Companies also need to take an increasing number of interests into consideration: political, ecological, ethical and financial demands increase. Organisations are expected to take care of their employees and be good corporate citizens. CSR (Corporate Social Responsibility) is one among many recent demands and expectations on organisations. The more dimensions and demands to consider, the more information and knowledge that is available and the tougher the competition, the more important it is to have talented people running organisations. State deregulation in many respects of the labour market (there has certainly been more regulation in other respect, e.g., more recently in the finance sector), particularly wage-setting, internationalisation (which, of course, embraces the labour market) and tough competition in consumer markets have made salaries and benefits more exposed to market forces. As a result, qualified employees in many industries can now earn a substantial wage premium, bigger than for several decades.

This development embraces society overall, and has important implications for most industries, employers, countries and jobs. Examples are numerous. The old distinction between blue-collar and white-collar workers becomes blurred. Car mechanics now need advanced computer skills for trouble shooting, and they must be prepared to discuss the often costly repairs with increasingly demanding customers. Car repair shops—at least authorised and bigger free-standing ones—are now clean, computerised environments, and many car dealership facilities now have glass doors between the customer face areas and the repair shop. Elevator repairer was once a job with a lot of freedom and little surveillance and control exercised by the office management. However, with new GPS technology, advanced repair equipment and a heavy pressure on efficiency and profitability, the situation has changed. After having implemented new systems, about half the old workforce decided to leave their employment at a major elevator manufacturer's after-sales service department: Efficiency improved by 50 to 100%[3]. Blue-collar workers are increasingly inclined to change job as their competence level increases, and they get better paid as the employer becomes more dependent upon them.

CONSUMERISATION OF THE LABOUR MARKET

To an increasing extent, young coworkers, influenced by emerging values in society, key elements in the popular culture and opportunities that new technology gives rise to, see work as a venue of self-realisation. This is certainly nothing new—Dutton (1994) suggested that:

> People are drawn to organisations that allow them to exhibit more of themselves and to enact a fuller range of characteristics and values in their self-concept. (Dutton, Dukerich, & Harquail, 1994, p. 244)

However, with Generation Y, the desire for self-realisation is much more clearly articulated. Generation Y individuals ask explicitly for self-realisation while the values of individuals born a few decades earlier suggested work to be done primarily for reasons of survival and supplying the family with food and other necessities, being a good citizen, get money to save for a rainy day, etc.

One could mistakenly suspect that Generation Y is a difficult group of people to deal with, since they put self-realisation as a top priority at work. However, unlike earlier generations, Generation Y individuals do not hide their values and ambitions: They want fun at work and they want to maximise life opportunities—but they nonetheless take work life seriously and will work hard to realise their ambitions to have a good career and a great CV. So how did these values emerge and get rooted in young individuals' set of values? As we will see, the answer lies in the society Generation Y individuals grew up in and the values society embraced, during the coming-of-age years particularly. The market environment, the social environment and inputs from the popular culture were different from what earlier generations experienced. That being said, blaming Generation Y for their values and behavioural traits is not a constructive approach, particularly not considering the fact that an individual cannot really help where she comes from, characteristics of her family and social setting or when she was born.

Many areas in life have been subject to consumerisation and the values that might be derived from the preferences and behavioural traits of individuals largely were created in consumer markets. Generation Y has an attitude to work that shows many similarities to values in consumer markets. As we will see, this put some particular demands on employers that want to attract Generation Y and make use of the advantages they might bring to the employer.

DISPOSITION OF THE BOOK

This introductory chapter has introduced the approach and theoretical assumptions of this book, and also tried to explain why there is a need for studies of Generation Y that deal with consumer and labour markets simultaneously.

Characteristics of Generation Y will be dealt with in Chapter 2. Generation Y will be defined and characteristics of Generation Y will be compared to other generations.

Chapter 3 will describe the role of society in forming generations. Values, the political climate, main events and changes in society along with other factors that influence a generational cohort will be dealt with.

Chapter 4 describes changes in the market environment and how competitive mechanisms influence supply and demand patterns, the number of choices available for individuals and how changes in state regulation, free trade, the emergence of low-cost production and international trade change cost structures and consumer choices.

Chapter 5 deals with the social environment—how individuals relate to each other and spend their leisure time. Ever since youth cultures emerged in the 1950s, individuals have spent a lot of time socialising and hanging out with friends. However, over time socialising and networking have undergone a transition from being a leisure time activity that primarily means relaxing and having fun to being an integrated part of an individual's social and professional plans for the future.

Chapter 6 discusses how Generation Y individuals behave as consumers and as coworkers. In this chapter, the foundation of Generation Y behaviour that has been dealt with in earlier chapters is manifested in more concrete behavioural traits and manners, important to e.g., primary health care, schools, universities and churches, to be able to compete successfully by designing strategies that appeal to Generation Y. This final chapter emphasises the consumerisation of the labour market that has been forced through in the era of the Generation Y cohort entering the labour market.

2 Generational Cohorts and the Emergence of Generation Y

In this chapter, Generation Y will be defined in relation to other generational cohorts. The underlying model used for doing this is the coming-of-age assumption, which suggests that a generational cohort is defined by the society she grew up in with a strong influence from cataclysmic events that take place before the age of about 23 years.

The very meaning of a generational perspective will be discussed in this chapter, and criticism against a focus on generations will be dealt with.

Moreover, characteristics of Generation Y will be dealt with based on an exposition on research on Generation Y. Other generations that will be treated include baby boomers (approximately 1945–1964); Generation X (approximately 1965–1978); and Generation Y (approximately 1979–1990). The generation coming after Generation Y will not be discussed extensively since definitions of non-mature fields may make the book appear dated when more solid definitions emerge. There is sufficient consensus about the definitions of baby boomers, Generation X and Generation Y, although there is limited consensus on where the generations start and end. Generations before the baby boomers, between baby boomers and Generation X, and after Generation Y have different names and there is little consensus on when they start and end.

Like in many other contexts where generational cohorts are discussed, this chapter will pay a lot of attention to baby boomers, a cohort that is often referred to in contrasting with Generation Y. One may wonder why baby boomers are used heavily as an illustration of a generational cohort that is inherently different from Generation Y. There are many reasons for this. First, both baby boomers and Generation Y are cohorts with a lot of research done that contribute to the analysis. Second, these cohorts are rather distinct as compared to the more vague definitions of cohorts in between boomers and Generation Y. Third, with an ambition to illustrate the transition from one society to another, avoiding the pitfall of being too detailed is likely to make the description more clearly articulated.

GENERATIONAL COHORTS AS SEGMENTATION VARIABLE

Finding groups or segments of consumers that have strong, homogeneous bonds is at the core of marketing thinking—ever since the early days of marketing, segmentation has been suggested to be the most important concept in marketing thinking. When similarities among a group of individuals exist, marketers can offer the same or very similar product, distribution and communications programme to a large number of consumers, and they are likely to respond in the way desired. Thus, segmentation is an effective approach that makes it possible for companies to reach their desired customers in a profitable way by designing the consumer offer in a way that fits the segment's characteristics.

Many segmentation approaches have long been known, including approaches that employ descriptive variables (e.g., demographic and geographic classification methods). Age has long been such a segmentation variable, but to get beyond the descriptive surface to understand motivations associated with age, cohorts have been found to be a superior concept (Meredith, Schewe, & Karlovich, 2002a). A cohort is a group of individuals who are born during roughly the same time period and travel through life together. They experience similar external events during their late adolescent/early adulthood years, approximately 17–23 years of age. The societal setting and defining moments that take place during these coming-of-age years influence individuals' values, preferences, attitudes and buying behaviour in ways that remain with them over their entire lifetime (Meredith & Schewe, 1994; Ryder, 1959/1985; Mannheim, 1952; Cutler, 1977; Rentz, Reynolds, & Stout, 1983; Rogler, 2002). Shared experiences during the highly influenceable coming-of-age years embed these values, or *cohort effects*. Research has shown that they remain relatively unchanged throughout life (Hill, 1970; Rogler & Cooney, 1984).

GENERATION OR GENERATIONAL COHORT?

Some researchers call marketing to birth groups *generational marketing*. However, it is important to note that cohorts and generations are not the same thing (cf. Markert, 2004). Each generation is defined by its years of birth. A *generation* is usually about 25 years in length, or roughly the time it takes a person to grow up and have children (Schewe & Meredith, 2004). Hence, with a life expectancy of about 80 years in most developed countries, there are three generations in existence at one time. A *generational cohort* can be as long or short as the external events which define it. A cohort defined by World War II, for example, may be only 6 years long (Schewe & Noble, 2000). Rather than using time of birth to determine different generations, generational cohorts are set apart by cataclysmic events that produce a change in the values, attitudes and predispositions in a society. Such secular change events create a discontinuous historical timeline, as suggested by Wahl:

> What is essential to the formation of a generational consciousness is some common frame of reference that provides a sense of rupture with the past and that will later distinguish the members of the generation from those who follow them in time. This frame of reference is always derived from great historical events like wars, revolutions, plagues, famines, and economic crises, because it is great historical events like these that supply the markers and signposts with which people impose order on their past and link their individual fates with those of the communities in which they live. (Wohl, 1979, p. 210)

Although there are conceptual differences between *generation* and *generational cohorts*, both concepts will be used in the book to represent a generational cohort. The multitude of definitions of cohorts, e.g., Generation X and baby boomers, makes it difficult to state that there is a generation, meaning the time it takes to grow up and have children, between each new generation. In most developed countries, people wait longer until they give birth to the next generation than before, and at the same time, baby boomers, Generation X and Generation Y cohorts are all less than 20 years in most definitions. Hence, what in everyday speech is called a generation resembles what has been referred to above as a generational cohort. It is rather unlikely, albeit possible, that a baby boomer has grandchildren belonging to the Generation Y cohort. The concept generation increasingly appears to describe a cohort and its characteristics based on an eclectic set of categories and aspects rather than a structured description of (as many sociologists would prefer to use the concept) how a generation inherits values from former generations and passes them on to the generations coming after them. For the specific purpose of this book, it is interesting to note that the Generation Y cohort is by many researchers, and also in our everyday dialogues, simply called "Generation Y", seldom "The Generation Y cohort".

THE COMING-OF-AGE ASSUMPTION

The notion of generational cohorts rests on the assumption that individuals were influenced by events occurring during their coming-of-age years. To validate this suggestion, it is important to investigate whether different cohorts really recall different events and experiences as influential in one's life. And if certain events were influential, when did they occur? A number of studies have dealt with this issue.

Schuman and Scott (1989) conducted a study which addressed these questions. They asked 1,410 Americans to recall three national and world events over the past 50 years that were especially important to them and tell why they were important. World War II and the Vietnam Conflict were mentioned most frequently by all age groups, however, an interesting pattern occurred. Individuals who were between 16 and 24 years old during World War II (1941–1945) and 15–27 years old during the Vietnam conflict (1965–1973) were significantly more likely to recall these events as being especially important to them. Schuman and Scott also found that individuals who experienced these events during their formative years (17 to 23 years of age) were able to cite personal experiences as reasons why these events were influential to them. Individuals who did not come of age during World War II or Vietnam were unable to give these kinds of accounts. Instead, they cited less personal reasons for the importance of these events. Schuman and Scott conclude by suggesting that since individuals that did not come of age during World War II or Vietnam could not attach personal meaning to these historical events, it is unlikely that their values, attitudes and behaviours were strongly influenced by them.

Similar patterns emerged for individuals' recollections of the Depression, advances in communication and transportation, John F. Kennedy's assassination, terrorism and nuclear weapons. Individuals who were in their 70s during the time of the study were the most likely to mention the Depression and advances in communication and transportation as influential to them. These individuals would have been in their teens and early 20s, i.e., their coming-of-age years, during these events. Additionally, this age group was able to give personal accounts of the Depression years, the development of the radio, television and jet airplanes. Similarly, individuals who would have been in their teens and early to mid-20s when Kennedy was assassinated in 1963 were the most likely to mention this event as influential. Finally, terrorism, which hit a high note in 1979 with the hostage crisis in Iran, was recalled most often by younger members of the sample who would have been in their late teens during that crisis. These younger individuals were also the most likely to cite nuclear weapons as important collective memories.

A Swedish study on individuals born in the 1980s (Söderqvist, 2010) suggests that one event has a unique position in shaping Generation Y—the 9/11 terror attack in New York. The second most important event referred to varies with the age of the interviewees: Those born in the early 1980s refer to the sinking of the Estonia ferry in September 1994, which claimed 852 lives and was the single deadliest shipwreck disaster in peacetime to have occurred in the Baltic Sea in recorded history.[1] Those born in the late 1980s recall December 2004 when Thailand's western coast was struck by the Boxing Day tsunami caused by the 2004 Indian Ocean earthquake as influential to them. The waves killed 543 Swedes and approximately 225,000 people in total.

Many people in the Generation Y cohort show strong feelings for Berlin, a strong representation of the end of the Cold War and the emergence of a united Europe. One third of Swedes born in the 1980s have a foreign background, meaning one or both parents are born in other countries than Sweden, which contributes to making this generational cohort more integrative and international than earlier generations.

SHARED EXPERIENCES

Not only do scholars that emphasise the coming-of-age years in the process of defining a generation emphasise the shared experiences that individuals of a particular generation go through. Already Mannheim (1952) in his classical work teaches that shared experience along biological or historical lines is possible, but not determined, in forming generations. Schuman and Scott (1989) clearly demonstrated that similarly aged individuals have similar memories. These memories are recalled predominantly from adolescence and young adulthood. Additionally, individuals appear to have personal experiences with the events that they cited, suggesting that these events are likely to influence them in the future.

Holbrook and Schindler (1989, 1994) illustrate the importance of young adulthood memories. They suggest that young adulthood experiences are likely to influence consumers well into their adulthood. Although "young adulthood" is defined fairly broadly, Holbrook and Schindler (1989) found that consumers are most prone to the socialisation of music around 23 years of age and movie stars at 14 years of age (Holbrook & Schindler, 1994). In a similar manner, the socialisation of preferences for apparel occurs in young adulthood. When asked to rate their preferences for pictures exemplifying various types of women's apparel over the decades, men showed the strongest preference for apparel that women were wearing when they—the men—were around 24 years of age (Schindler & Holbrook, 1993).

Cohort effects appear to be life-long effects. They provide the communality for each cohort being targeted as a separate group or segment, and this appears to apply in consumer markets as well as in labour markets. Since these cohorts can be described by the ages of their constituents, they offer an especially rich vehicle for understanding differences across generations.

The existence of cohorts has been found in numerous developed countries, too (Meredith et al., 2002; Meredith, Schewe, Hiam, & Karlovich, 2002; Schewe & Meredith, 2004; Hung, Gu, & Yim, 2007; Dou, Wang, & Zhou, 2006; Parment, 2008; Chaston, 2009; Parment, 2009c). With the perspective taken here, it is the nature of the defining moments within these other cultures that defines the topography of the cohort terrain. Different defining moments create cohorts with different dates, different lengths and different values. For instance, Germany, Russia and Sweden have experienced many events of social consequence, different from those that took place in the U.S., while at various times have been affected by events that had similar consequences, e.g., the Cold War and the end of it.

CRITICISM AGAINST A GENERATIONAL
COHORT PERSPECTIVE

There are many ways in which a generational cohort perspective might be criticised. Here, some of the reasons that may be brought against a generational cohort perspective will be discussed briefly.

A generational cohort might be best understood by understanding its relation to other generational cohorts (Bergqvist, 2009; Grenier, 2007). Grenier (2007) suggests that the ways older and younger poeple relate to each other holds the potential for conflict—or connection—between generations. However, as is suggested by Grenier, an inherent conflict rests in understanding other generations: Older people have been young, but this does not apply the other way. Moreover, it is reasonable to assume that some older people would prefer to be younger than they actually are, and this may bias analyses and interpretations. Some researchers have focused on conducting research with older people (e.g., Gubrium & Sankar, 1994; Lawton & Herzog, 1989) but as suggested by Grenier (2007), the way age and generation influence the interpretation of social phenomenon may produce intergenerational conflict or connection.

In the last decades, there has been an increasing fluidity of the life course (Featherstone & Hepworth, 1991; Gilleard & Higgs, 2000). This transition is linked to other changes in society. Also conceptualisations of family have been subject to increasing fluidity. As put by Parry (2005), notions of family are not static, but rather a fluid process subject to interpretation and re-evaluation as a result of life events. Ecclestone, Biesta, & Hughes (2009) suggest fluidity to characterise students in dealing with different domains and stages of their lives. Ecclestone et al. even suggest that fluidity is needed in a postmodern society. An increasing fluidity makes it increasingly difficult to frame in and interpret phenomena, e.g., comparing family impact on decision making among older and younger individuals when the concept of family is subject to fluidity. Older and younger will have different interpretations of the concept of family, which makes it difficult to compare the results, at least unless the researcher is highly aware of this. On the other hand, generational cohort effects appear to transcend professions, sexes, nations and cultures, particularly so in a globalised world.

Mannheim (1952) suggested that the boundaries of generational experience may be socially and culturally influenced, something that might be seen as a restriction to the explanatory power of generational cohorts in forecasting behaviour and setting up models that deal with the interplay between a number of variables. However, most phenomena studied in the social sciences—not least in management and marketing—are influenced by social and cultural factors. It is up to the researcher whether those sort of aspects are taken into account in research design and model specifications. This book attempts to understand the Generation Y cohort, while considering the substantial differences that—within a given cohort—exist across countries, cultures, sexes, metropolitan versus rural areas, etc. Generational cohort effects are assumed to be strong, however, in many situations other effects might be even stronger.

To make a qualified analysis in a given situation, having knowledge about not only what influences consumer behaviour (or any other thing that needs a deeper understanding), but also the interplay between variables, is an analytical advantage. For instance, in many countries there are vast differences between metropolitan and rural areas (cf. Bergqvist, 2009; Parment, 2008a, 2009a, 2009c), and these differences may be stronger than the cohort effects. Changes and emerging values, attitudes and behavioural traits take off in metro areas and then there is a diffusion pattern that embraces city areas first, then rural areas and finally (if ever) remote areas[2]. As we will see, the differences across areas appear to be more limited with Generation Y than in earlier generations, but they are still vast in many contexts. Similar to generational cohort effects, urbanisation patterns and attitudes in metro and rural areas are patterns (Bergqvist, 2009), which may be stronger in some situations than in others. For instance, there is probably a stronger cohort difference in clothing style between baby boomer and Generation Y teachers—the former more formally dressed and the latter strongly influenced by different elements in the popular culture— than between baby boomer and Generation Y lawyers. But the pattern of change is still strong. Generation Y lawyers are more likely to be dressed down during leisure time and while still adhering to the code of conduct of the profession have a different attitude, meaning they are not inherently convinced that lawyers must be dressed in suits.

A strong attitude in the popular culture to promote metro areas, e.g., in *Sex and the City*, while other movies, sitcoms, etc., portray living in rural areas as very boring, cf. the movie *Show Me Love*, a Swedish movie about a rural place called Åmål, which has taught many young individuals to move out from rural areas. While the original name of the rural town was kept in Germany—*Raus aus Åmål*—the movie was presented under the title *Show Me Love* or *Descrubiendo el amor* to viewers in many countries. Moreover, the emergence of the Internet, a significant increase in the number of tv programmes on fashion and beauty (e.g., *Project Runway*), and an emerging multitude of fashion magazines available at low prices have brought metro, city, rural and remote areas closer to each other. But one thing has not changed: It is still the metro areas that largely define good taste, new trends and scan the international environment—which should not come as a surprise. Moreover, metro areas have many international guests. The analysis will benefit from understanding these different dimensions. In consumer marketing, generational cohorts is one segmentation variable, and depending on the situation at hand, the cohorts effect might be stronger or weaker than other segmentation effects, i.e., demographic and psychographic effects.

DISTINCTNESS OF GENERATIONAL COHORTS

Needless to say, the changes that came with the Generation Y cohort did not occur over one night. The preferences and behavioural traits of Generation Y emerged during a period of several years, and, like many changes in society, the patterns were different in metropolitan and rural areas; across people with different education and training; and the patterns differed across countries. Many changes occur in metropolitan areas before they spread to city areas, and then to rural areas, and these diffusion patterns appear to apply also onto the change of generations.

Even a person born in the late 1960s may perceive herself as a Generation Y, and may even share values and behavioural traits with Generation Y individuals. However, there are some values that a 1960s individual hardly can share with her two decades younger colleague, and there are nuances in experiences, language, the relation to big events, political happenings and disasters that speak against the individual's argument to be part of another generation. A toddler whose father left the country for 3 years to work as a soldier in Afghanistan or Vietnam has an experience that is difficult to neglect—it ultimately influences the way the individual approaches parents, authorities and war movies. Individuals who experienced the Great Depression in the 1930s, or suffered heavily in the financial crises in the early 1990s or late 2000s when people used to high living standards had to leave their homes, are more sensitive to signs of risk exposure and more likely to save for a rainy day—they know they could come. An individual who experienced 9/11, the fall of the Franco dictatorship in Spain or the Chernobyl disaster is likely to be affected by that—forever!

The argument sometimes brought that not everybody fits into a generational cohort is worth commenting on. Most if not all categorisations used in the social sciences are characterised by a lack of ability to predict the behaviour of every single person under every circumstance. There are people living in the countryside whose lifestyle and consumer behaviour is similar to that normally associated with metropolitan areas. There are private owned and run hospitals that act like public hospitals. There are males with a shopping style normally associated with females, etc. Nonetheless, from an aggregated perspective, patterns of behaviour of the majority in a cohort are helpful for forecasting behavioural patterns.

NOW WE WILL TAKE OFF:
THE EMERGENCE OF GENERATION Y

Just like for previous generations, such as Generation X, there are different definitions of Generation Y. This book is a contribution to this discussion, without claiming to provide a final definition—that ambition would be difficult to fulfill.

Based on the discussion above and the assumptions being stated, it is now time to define Generation Y. Generation X includes people born in the 1960s and '70s, ending in the late 1970s to around 1980. Generation X was introduced to a broader public as a rather negative concept in the early 1990s. The term was popularised by Douglas Coupland's 1991 novel, *Generation X: Tales for an Accelerated Culture*, concerning young adults during the late 1980s and their lifestyles. The term Generation X was coined by the Magnum photographer Robert Capa already in the early 1950s. Capa said: "We named this unknown generation, The Generation X, and even in our first enthusiasm we realised that we had something far bigger than our talents and pockets could cope with" (MacAllister & Harris, 2003, p. 5). Subsequent appearances of the term in the mid-1960s and mid-1970s narrowed the scope for Generation X from Capa's global generation to a focus on mainstream, rather prosperous, Western individuals.

Many believed that Generation X would refuse traditional core elements such as parents, family and work by not seeing it as a duty. Traditional institutions (marriage, family, etc.) were questioned by Generation X. Now similar attitudes towards Generation Y may be identified, but they often lack a solid foundation. Generation Y employees may show up late at work sometimes, and take the opportunity to leave early when there is an option to do so, but that does not mean they are lazy, and they are likely to put in much energy and many hours when there is a need to. There are many reports on how much time young employees particularly spend on Facebook and other Internet platforms, which transforms into huge amounts of money lost for employers. However, many web pages update the content automatically. An employee arriving at the office at 9:15 and opening three Internet pages may be suspected of surfing for hours, although only a few minutes were spent on surfing the web. The IT office doesn't know whether the employee updated the page or if it was automatically updated, but still writes reports to top management on employees' extensive Internet usage. And young employees who don't like to be in meetings and avoid joining them may make a significant contribution to the organisation's effectiveness—however, at the same time, they give older colleagues another argument for stating that young colleagues are lazy, unwilling to take responsibility and reluctant to be part of shared activities.

CHANGES THAT COME WITH GENERATION Y

In this section, we will discuss changes and transitions that are strongly intertwined with the emergence of Generation Y. A common statement is that Generation Y is technology savvy and "digital natives": Having grown up with the Internet and the opportunities and challenges it entails, they are more used to computers and they do not have any significant problems in using new technology to execute work more effectively and efficiently than generations before them. However, although it is difficult to argue against the suggestion that this generation has a natural ability to deal with the latest technology, one may question whether the high level of technology familiarity and savvyness is really defining a generation. In actual fact, many individuals born in the 1940s and 1950s are very familiar with computers and the latest technological devices, and even Generation Xers, born in the 1960s and the 1970s, learned to know computers and advanced technological solutions before or during their coming of age years in the 1980s and 1990s.

We will now define a number of other characteristics that define Generation Y and a pattern of the Generation Y cohort as a distinct generation will emerge.

SOCIALISATION PATTERNS

A central theme in understanding generations is socialisation patterns. As discussed above, older colleagues may react towards the attitude of many Generation Y individuals to be reluctant to having many meetings in the workplace or showing up early and leaving late only for reasons of being less senior. The patterns of socialisation change over time, so when Generation Y individuals appear to socialise less with colleagues—fewer and shorter meetings, coffee breaks on the go instead of sitting down and reluctance to staying late at work unless necessary—they socialise with their friends (like any generation, although Generation Y appears to have more friends than earlier generations; this theme is thoroughly discussed in Chapter 5), but more with alumni friends, career networks, former colleagues, etc. As Generation Y individuals change jobs more often and plan to do so also in the future, they find stronger reasons to build their network independently from their current workplace. Important to note: It is a myth that Generation Y in general is planning to change jobs very often and are unwilling to stay with the same employer for a number of years. If they find the job appealing and if there are adequate opportunities to make a career within the organisation, they are likely to stay. But their threshold for changing jobs is lower and organisations must work harder to make sure Generation Y individuals like the work environment. Although great employers will still get many qualified employees who stay with the employer for several years, from an aggregate perspective, Generation Y individuals will change jobs more often and have a smaller part of their social networks in the current workplace compared to earlier generations. And they will have great use of their social networks in getting inspiration, performing work assignments, selling products, creating new projects and ventures and recruiting new coworkers when they are in the position to do that.

MANY CHOICES INCREASE DEMANDS

Generation Y is used to having many opportunities but are not stressed by it—as opposed to baby boomers, who grew up and lived a great part of their lives in a society with relatively few choices. Over time, the number of choices people are used to has gradually increased, and the level of opportunities that individuals find natural has increased accordingly.

The high level of choices Generation Y individuals are used to does not mean they are not stressed—it's other things that bother and stress them. They have to focus on choices that are important to them—where to live, whom to spend time with, whether to, what subject area and where to study and what to buy. The latter certainly applies to so-called high-involvement products, which are characterised by a high degree of buyer involvement in the purchase process. Products like insurances, finance and electricity remain low-involvement products and have little or nothing to do with an individual's social profile or self-realisation (Parment & Söderlund, 2010). Thus, such products are not crucial choices but like any generation, Generation Y wants to make good deals and their limited loyalty makes them inclined to use Internet and other services that help them spend as little as possible on these things. That gives room for more spending on emotional and self-realisation consumption. However, low involvement products may still enjoy a rather high degree of what appears to be loyalty, but it is not

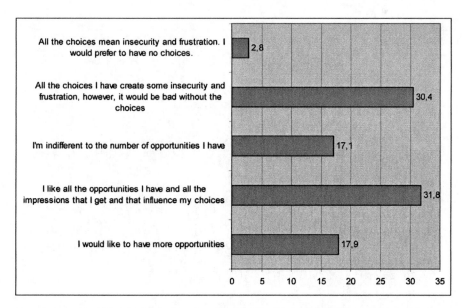

Figure 2.1   Only 2.8% of Generation Y individuals would prefer to have no choices. 17.9% would like to have even more opportunities. Figures in percent. Source: Generation Y survey.

true loyalty but rather repeat purchasing, typical of low involvement products (cf. Jensen & Hansen, 2008). For low involvement products, the buyer's interest in finding new, better choices is limited.

One example of something that is stressing older individuals more than young individuals is (unanswered) e-mails. Older individuals are used to, and have grown up with, values that suggest that one should answer every incoming inquiry or question addressed to him or her. When leaving the office on Friday afternoon, the ideal with earlier generations is to have no unanswered e-mails and a clean office table. Generation Y knows that it is hardly possible to answer every e-mail while at the same time reaching other goals in work life. They will certainly answer important e-mails but many are also seen as opportunities and options. Being used to information overload may be an advantage in work life and other contexts with information processing, since it makes the individual faster in distinguishing between spam and information relevant for the decision making at hand.

Generation Y individuals are more responsible for developing their own life and career strategies than earlier generations. There are more opportunities now and career patterns are not as linear as they used to be. Moreover, studies suggest that they are stressed by getting stuck with the same employer and 17% of Young Professionals say that they apply for a new job "to see whether I'm hot stuff in the labour market" (Universum, 2009). As shown in Figure 2.2, only 2% of Generation Y individuals are really worried about their capacity in relation to today's labour market and its

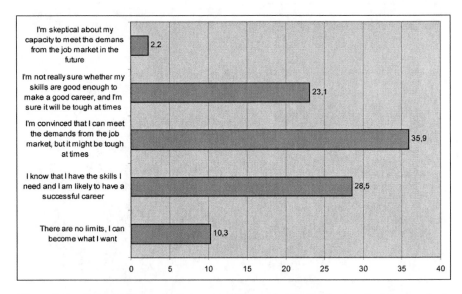

Figure 2.2   Only 2.2% are really worried about their capacity in relation to today's labour market and its demands. 10.3% state that there are no limits—they can become whatever they want. Figures in percent. Source: Generation Y survey.

demands. One out of 10 state that there are no limits—they can become whatever they want to.

The labour market is undergoing a fundamental change with more power to the employee, more market forces and, to sum up the development, a consumerisation of the labour market. This reflects a reorientation in the way employees market themselves to, and how employers respond to, choosing workplace, something natural for the Generation Y cohort.

Generation Y feels some pressure to make a good career and trusting the employer, the state or somebody else appears to be a strategy that might have worked a couple of decades ago, but hardly in the future. Thus, the results should be interpreted in light of a high awareness among Generation Y that they are responsible for developing their careers. It is nonetheless interesting to see how well they appear to adapt to the current circumstances. Having grown up in a society that focuses on opportunities and choices, they have learned from early years that they can realise their goals, if they really try to. They may change opinion later in life, but starting the career with a positive view on future opportunities is likely to be a strong driving force that, in combination with their more direct way of communicating (more on this in Chapter 6), will vitalise many organisations and industries.

Survey studies are subject to a number of limits and sometimes respondents (consciously or unconsciously) fill in the survey as a representation of whom they want to be rather than whom they are (cf. Deshpande, 1983; Scandura, 2000). That should be considered in interpreting the data. However, several forces in the market environment support the development towards more choices, and the effects described here. Labour market data support the idea that people change jobs more often than before: There is little aggregated data on this, but many industry region or country specific data that support this idea, and very little speaks against it. Anecdotal evidence from many industries and interview data with few exceptions support this trend. Data collected in the research projects that lay the foundation of this book unequivocally support the idea that individuals change jobs more often, as part of an ideology with a strong focus on one's own career.

So far, a few examples of Generation Y characteristics have been given. In the following chapters we will study Generation Y from a society level (Chapter 3), from the perspective of the market environment (Chapter 4), from the social environment perspective (Chapter 5), and how the characteristics and forces that can be derived from these three highly interrelated spheres are manifested in how Generation Y behaves as consumers and coworkers (Chapter 6).

3   Generation Y and Society
Values and Defining Moments

This chapter describes the role of society in forming generations. Values, the political climate, main changes in society and other factors that influence a generation will be dealt with. Research from sociology and marketing will be used in framing in the context that shaped the values of Generation Y, with many references to baby boomers, a generational cohort that in many respects provides an interesting contrast to Generation Y. Key elements of society, e.g., individualism versus collectivism; the attention society pays to institutions and authorities; voluntarism versus determinism, etc., contribute to the analysis of societal elements and forces that lay the foundation of how individuals' attitudes and behavioural traits are developed. All of these factors influence the society that individuals grow up and come of age in.

There has been a strong division between the consumption sphere and working life. Modernistic societies emerged and grew under a strong influence from values of reason rather than emotions, and leisure time was seen as a necessary break to charge the batteries physically and emotionally, thus being prepared to come back to work as a highly productive individual, a key player in the creation of wealthy, prospering nations.

Over time, the division between work and leisure time has become blurred, the state has lost its influence on individuals, traditional authorities have lost their power and values of self-realisation together with an extensive period of youth have contributed to attitudinal transitions among people. Generation Y grew up with commercial television, high economic standards and few or no memories of the Cold War and financial crises, thus reflecting a set of values that formed the attitudes of this generation in a manner fundamentally different from what characterised the society that earlier generations grew up in. For instance, Meredith and Schewe (1994) suggest that the generation before baby boomers have little debt and apply the principle of saving for a rainy day.

Society experienced many changes during Generation Ys coming of age. This chapter will lay out the foundation of the societal level in the model that the book is based on. Defining moments and other major events have contributed significantly to changes in values at a societal level. This has, as we will see in later chapters, important implications for how individuals approach consumption and work.

MAJOR EVENTS AND TRENDS IN THE 1990s AND 2000s

Every generational cohort is programmed from the moment of birth, and Generation Y began a series of programming experiences when they were infants back in the 1980s. The coming-of-age assumption holds that the entire early life cycle shapes a generation's values and behavioural traits, with a strong influence during the years from 17 to 23.

Trends and changes seldom have a precise date, and the Generation Y cohort represents individuals with at least a decade span in their birth date. An individual born in 1980 is shaped by a different set of external events compared to somebody who was born in 1989. All major events and trends that are discussed in this chapter do not have the specific power of a defining moment, however, they have strongly influenced the society in which Generation Y grew up. When taken together, a picture emerges of a society that is inherently different in many key aspects to the society that earlier generational cohorts grew up in.

The most influential years for Generation Y as a whole are the '90s and the '00s, but also some events and trends that emerged in the 1980s will be discussed, since they grew important during the '90s and '00s. Some of the changes are rather obvious, e.g., that Generation Y is the first generation to grow up surrounded by the Internet and new tools to communicate and make friends: Mobile phones and a multitude of tv channels became available to just about everybody. But there are other more fundamental shifts in society that may be derived from less obvious events and trends. And, needless to say in the book's third chapter, many of the characteristics, changes and driving forces dealt with are highly interrelated.

CHANGES IN POPULAR CULTURE

During Generation Y's teenage and coming-of-age years, they witnessed many changes in the popular culture. New television programmes gave new perspectives on life. This change was strongest in, e.g., Eastern Europe, where the television had been state-controlled. Opportunities to take part of a Western lifestyle were limited. In these countries, democratisation, market forces and the opportunity to adapt to a Western-oriented lifestyle with consumption at the heart of the desired living patterns came largely at the same time. In, e.g., Scandinavia, television was also to a high extent state-owned but showed a selection of partly harmful, partly harmless television programmes from the U.S. and Western Europe—*Dallas* and the *Dynasty* were shown in these countries and later in the 1980s *Cosby* and

Seinfeld. At the end of the 1980s, the state eased control in many countries and gave room for commercial television channels. In the 1990s, most major programmes were available throughout the Western world. A multitude of programmes were now available: MTV made pop music videos available around the clock; sitcoms, e.g., *Seinfeld* and *Frasier*; talk shows with Johnny Carson, David Letterman and Jay Leno; and programmes that promoted a glamorous lifestyle, e.g., *Sex and the City*, emerged. The latter particularly appears to have a strong impact on Generation Y's values. In interviews there are many references to *Sex and the City*; *Beverly Hills, 90210;* and later *Gossip Girl* and *The Hills*, to name a few but significant television programmes. In a relatively short time period, a glamorous lifestyle and a desire to live such a life became available to teenagers and young adults across the Western world, and soon also to other parts of the world.

THE WESTERN WORLD STILL DOMINATES
THE CONSUMPTION AND CULTURE SPHERES

Diffusion patterns vary across continents and countries but the dominance of a Western-oriented consumption-based culture is strong also in parts of the world with other traditions, other perspectives on the state, on religion, etc. In Thailand, for instance, not only international hotel chains but also major upmarket shopping malls, where many locals are shopping, are representing a Western lifestyle. With the exception of a few department stores selling Thai products, the majority of the supplied goods is Western brands or Western-styled goods. And with very few exceptions, fashion and style magazines are all Asian versions of European and U.S. magazines translated into the local language with no or few other modifications.

The current global development appears to move the industrial and economic power from the formerly dominating U.S. and Europe to China and the Middle East. Many U.S. and European companies have been acquired by owners from Russia, the Middle East and China. With the Asian and Middle East economies getting stronger, while the U.S. and several European countries are having severe financial problems, at least with regard to state budgets, trade (im)balances and budget deficits, the direction for the future seems to be clear. However, with regard to consumption culture, the Western world still has a very strong impact. When asked to name leading Chinese companies and ministers, like the generations before them, most Generation Y individuals have very little knowledge. So although an increasing part of the products we buy are developed and manufactured in these emerging countries (which is now the wrong expression for countries like China and India!) they are dominating economies, not emerging ones. Despite this, the knowledge stays very much with what happens in the Western world. This particularly holds for the popular culture, with an extensive flow of tv programmes from the Western world to emerging countries, but hardly any flow back. The same holds for fashion clothing and other lifestyle products. It has been proven that many Asian consumers admire premium products from Europe particularly (Batra, Ramaswamy, Alden, Steenkamp, & Ramachander, 2000; Park, Rabolt, & Jeon, 2008; Zhou & Hui, 2003).

A MARKET-BASED IDEOLOGY MEANS MANY CHOICES—AND A NEW SET OF ATTITUDES

The number of choices is largely a function of market characteristics, but also a question of the attitudes of individuals who make decisions in consumer markets or any other context where there are choices to be made. Over time the number of choices have undoubtedly increased in most life spheres, and this development is largely driven by changes in the market environment, which will be dealt with in the next chapter. However, there are many other driving forces than those derived from the market environment. Here, a number of central driving forces in the development towards a market-based ideology will be suggested and explained.

- *Political deregulation* as part of a more market-oriented ideology, often called *New Public Management (NPM)*. This approach, which emerged in the 1980s promoted by, e.g., Teacher and Reagan, suggests that to deal with increased demands on effectiveness and efficiency from politicians, and a changed citizen attitude with higher demands and also wishes to customise public services, the public sector must use government and control mechanisms, ideas and tools from the private sector (cf. Ferlie et al., 1996; Hood, 1995; Schedler, 2006). This changed political ideology, which to a varying extent influenced the entire Western world, resulted in tax authorities with 24/7 telephone service, private and independently owned Kindergarten in countries that used to let the state run child care, universities competing on state resources instead of just getting them, outsourcing of services that the public sector used to perform so running a public hospital became a coordination of the core activities performed in-house and transportation companies, restaurants and cleaning services bought in the open, external market. Politicians promoted *the power of citizens choosing*, an ideology that came from the private sector, which constituted a dramatic contrast to the old ideology of the state choosing and taking care of its citizens, something citizens were used to as it was the natural state of things.
- *Internationalisation* meant, in addition to the abundance of product and services offers that came with Internationalisation, that individuals became more open to new ideas and discovered food, cultures and

leisure activities: The latter is a concept that does not really apply to Generation Y, a generation that is doing all sorts of activities regardless of whether it is at work or during leisure time. Cheap travel and more students studying abroad (later, the study abroad ratio didn't increase anymore but reached a stable level, however, at the time, it increased) broadened perspectives.

- *Cable and satellite television* moved the power of choice to citizens and the television stars, and not only increased the supply of television programmes but also introduced a strong intrachannel competition on viewers. Financed by television commercials the channels created tools to attract the desired viewers and thus maximise income from commercials. The television stars became very important and particularly many American television stars with hundreds of millions of regular viewers all over the world—Sarah Jessica Parker, Jerry Seinfeld, Larry King, David Letterman, Kelsey Grammer, Oprah Winfrey, Jennifer Aniston and Jay Leno to mention a few—became very popular. These individuals—and the focus on individual actors, etc.—were key to the success of sitcoms and other programmes that generated income for the channels, and new customers for the companies that bought the commercials. Television stars became the new superstars and earned a lot more money than traditional rock and movie stars. Ever since the days of Friends comedy stars might earn up to, and even more than, $1 million an episode while the drama top earners earn around $400,000 an episode (Battaglio, 2010). Over time the opportunities to get access to music without paying for it have increased and accordingly the income of musicians, once enjoying high and stable income, decreased. It didn't start with the Internet in the 1990s but rather earlier with compact tape recorders, etc., but really took off with CD burners, Kazaa, Direct Connect and later YouTube. The new superstars were television stars and, as we will discuss later in this chapter, the supermodel, who also appeared in sitcoms and talk shows.
- A crucial driving force here is the emergence of a new type of *reality television* in the late 1990s, with *Survivor/Robinson* (1997), *American Idol* (2002), *America's Next Top Model* (2003), *Project Runway* (2004), *The Apprentice* (2004) and *Big Brother* (1997) as significant and well-known examples of reality television programmes that have been exported to many countries: They all had a global effect, having each been successfully syndicated in dozens of countries. In these programmes, the format is decided top-down but the content by the real people who participate in the programme. Strange and weird characters may not only have a place but also contribute to making the programmes very popular. Anyone can succeed provided a sufficient level of talent and luck are at hand—it is not like in earlier generations, when coming from the right family or knowing the right people might have been necessary to succeed.

• The new opportunities described here combined with a *different approach to raising children* contributed to transfer a new set of values (raising children is to a large extent guided by values in society) to the new generation that grew up. Interviews with baby boomers suggest that parents of Generation Y have contributed to children's self-realisation at an early stage (Parment, 2008d). For instance, the attitude on watching television gradually moved from something that would be dangerous for children to an integrated part of life and it has even been suggested that watching television (not any programme, of course!) may be good for children's development. In interviews, European baby boomers, regardless of whether they grew up in a situation of scarcity or come from a wealthy family, state that they were forced not to throw away things they could eat or use again. "I grew up after WWII and although my father was a senior bank executive, my parents and society overall emphasised the need for caring about scarce resources, being a good and well-behaved citizen and contribute to building society after the war. Self-realisation was not a theme at the time" (female, born 1946). That is one among many changes in the attitude and practice that have changed in the last decades.

Arguments may be put against each of the driving forces suggested above. For instance, the critical volume of running a viable business has increased in many industries, thus making it more difficult to run a company that provides local services for the public sector as suggested by the New Public Management approach. Or, the environmental and antiglobalisation movements' negative impact on international trade. There has definitely been many contramovements against Internationalisation, one of the most significant being nationalistic political movements, e.g., Jörg Heider's FPD in Austria. Reality television may be seen as a trend in popular culture rather than part of a bigger change, etc. However, the intentions of political deregulation were clear: Focus on efficiency and more power to citizens. And the effect of this and the other changes described above was that markets, cultures and individuals were more oriented towards markets and choices in the marketplace as opposed to the state taking care of, and making decisions for, individuals. Taken together these driving forces fundamentally changed society for most people. And Generation Y individuals particularly grew up with another set of values than their parents, since the significant changes and events happened before or during Generation Y's coming-of-age years.

The changes described above have been stronger in many European countries than in the U.S.—the latter often being portrayed as a country of opportunities—but also American citizens experience an increase in the number of real choices. Moreover, Internationalisation has contributed to Americans questioning choices that earlier appeared natural, while at the same time new opportunities have emerged.

BEING ONE'S OWN ENTREPRENEUR—A LIFE STRATEGY FOR GENERATION Y

As an effect of all the changes described above, an increased interest among Generation Y to create new ventures has been noticed in many countries (cf. international entrepreneurship indices and public labour market data). This reflects a reorientation among young individuals from big companies and institutions—working at Siemens, IKEA, IBM, Air France, British Telecom or the Foreign Ministry used to be the dream of young people—to being one's own entrepreneur. Rankings suggest that many Generation Y individuals and Young Professionals still want to work for big organisations, which put a lot more effort into building their employer brands than smaller organisations. By its very nature, a big organisation gests more ideal employer preferences due to its size and higher brand awareness. Generation Y individuals will change jobs more often and have a more positive attitude towards starting a new venture. Their career strategies are more focused on self-realisation and staying competitive in the labour market, than on one-firm commitment, which was a strong preference among baby boomers and also a significant part of Generation X individuals. This change appears to be strongly inspired by the changes and reorientations described in this chapter.

The decreasing loyalty that increasingly characterises the labour market has its roots in the strong consumption culture with all choices and—to approach it from the positive side—opportunities that it offers. A few decades ago there were far fewer choices in life. There were fewer choices with regard to telephone operators, educational programmes (one studied law, theology or engineering, without a multitude of mixed or customised programmes), car models or places to go during the vacation. The Internet didn't exist, and price comparisons were difficult to run. Calling 10 retailers would take a lot of time and that in combination with a dominating local mindset gave a preference for local suppliers.

An important driving force in the transition from loyalty as a rule to a new approach where choosing became a natural part of citizens' way-of-thinking is the Globalisation of tastes and preferences, with strong influences from the popular culture and consumption cultures. In the 1980s, lifestyle consumption became influential and brands could now reach an iconic status, meaning consuming the brand contributes to the consumer's self-expression and personal identity. To reach an iconic status, the brand must fabricate a meaningful storytelling and represent a cultural contradiction, a mismatch between prevailing ideology and emergent undercurrents in society (Holt, 2004). This obviously meant a contrast to the focus on product functionality that was prevailing at the time.

The combination of a number of societal changes gave room for a lifestyle focus which reflected an orientation away from functionalistic, modernistic societies to a new postmodernistic era of lifestyle and attitude focus, a fragmentation in consumer preferences and an emerging focus on individuals' self-realisation. Howard Schultz, president, CEO, and chairman of Starbucks, describes it in the following way: "A great brand raises the bar—it adds a greater sense of purpose to the experience, whether it's the challenge to do your best in sports and fitness, or the affirmation that the cup of coffee you're drinking really matters" (this statement is quoted in, and criticised by, Morris, 2001). Who had thought about the Internet and all that it brings, companies that implement all-embracing corporate identity programmes and politics who deregulate markets to make room for citizen choices and entrepreneurial activity.

FROM LACK OF INFORMATION TO INFORMATION OVERLOAD

A defining characteristic of the emerging society is *information overload*. Generation Y grew up in a society of plenty of information and scarcity of time for most people—and the tendency has grown stronger day by day. While companies earlier had coworkers that extracted and compiled information, coworkers who selected and sorted information have gradually taken over. This fundamental change in society may not be fully considered or even known by professionals, managers and others who are expected to be in tune with the world around. Not even students—although they are aware of the new society since it's so obvious to them—are getting material that reflect what is going on.

Generation Y individuals know that all choices must not be made, and it is difficult to base every decision made on genuine research—there are too many matters and too much information out there. For instance, their way of dealing with e-mails—something that may be restricted by certain rules in the workplace—is likely to be different from how earlier generations dealt with it. Offers from telephone and broadband companies, direct marketing and the overload of tv channels, news, etc.—there are many areas in life that are significantly influenced by the changes that Generation Y contribute to realising. While former generations selected and stored information, afraid of not getting access to it again, Generation Y is more relaxed and realise that they can't obtain every available piece of information.

A critical attitude and an automatic selection of relevant information are inherent attitudes of individuals growing up in a society of information overload. As a contrast, a baby boomer who is plagued by the information overload—"I find it very difficult, it takes a lot of time, and it is difficult to select and choose. Every day, there is new information, where should I have my priorities?"—has an approach to information that would hardly be found with younger generational cohorts. She and her 70-year-old husband mark newspapers and direct marketing after they have been read through, and they both emphasise how stressed they are after a week away. "It's so

Box 3.1   Dated Textbooks and Study Material
            Present a Wrong Picture of Society

One of the most used textbooks in the field of Management Control is Anthony and Govindarajan's *Management Control Systems. Text and Cases*, issued 2007 in its 12th edition. It is a classical, American textbook with a clear structure and a rather narrow perspective of the subject area it covers—how companies can design control systems that implement the intended strategies. Inspired by professor Anthony's Harvard School approach, the textbook is based on many cases, which teach students key learnings in a structured way, with illustrations of problems from real companies which students have to solve.

Through updated and instructive Instructor's Manuals, teachers can follow the development of the book's content and cases. In some instances, the authors have developed the thinking and reasoning behind cases, e.g., in a case on an ice cream company (originally named Midwest Ice Cream, created by Shank and Rauwerdink, 1974, later Boston Creamery). The control system was presented as a great and sound system in the 1970s but later, in the 1990s, the very same system was criticised by the authors and used as an example of a control system that appears to be sound, but has inherent flaws.

Teachers with a lot of work to do and hence limited opportunities to spend time on understanding what is going on in society may have limited reflections and learnings on management control systems beyond changes that are presented in new issues of the course literature. However, collating the 11th (2002) and 12th (2007) reveals very few changes in terms of the text content. The publisher promises over 40 current real-world examples to have been added throughout the text, and six brand-new cases that address core dilemmas of management control. Moreover, in the book of almost 800 pages, the publisher promises the elimination of 10 cases that have gone out of date since the 11th edition.

Surprisingly, one of the cases that remains in the 12th edition from 2007 is Galvor Company, a 1973 case about an American company that acquires a French subsidiary. About 40 coworkers at the French operation work in the Accounting Department, which compiles financial reports. Only one of them speaks English. Today, the company would have nobody compiling reports since it would all be computer-based, but there would be a need for a few people who select the important information and analyse data and information from the control system. Students Taking a 2011 module in Management Control might learn from the case if a point is made of the dated approach on information processing. If the case is presented as reflecting current practice, as suggested by the publisher, students are likely to, and should, experience the study material as unmodern.

There are many generic problems in organisations that are largely the same as 1973 so old cases and articles may be highly applicable. For instance, Teodor Levitt's *Marketing Myopia* (1961) is still used in many Marketing course modules and it provides many learning insights. However, if an area of significant technological progress, as is the case of information technology, is presented, students should be made aware about current practice.

Box 3.2   Not in Tune with Times—Storing and Indexing Without Meaning

At the turn of the millennium, a baby boomer professor at the University of South Australia spent a large part of every workday on archiving and indexing scientific articles that he found interesting and, to make it accessible in the future, those articles should be stored in a database for future use. The professor was frustrated with the increasing supply of scientific journals and articles, which day by day increased the complexity and intensity of his work with the database.

It is unclear why the professor was allowed to work with the offline database. All articles were available online already at the time, and search engines improve day by day.

Many people can understand the frustration of the professor: The amount of information available increases, and it becomes increasingly difficult to keep control about everything that goes on within one's field of expertise. For Generation Y—and certainly many others—information overload is the norm.

much to go through when we come back. My husband reads all newspapers, I do the direct marketing". This highly educated couple of early baby boomers (the husband is actually even older) are used to having the opportunity to deal with every new information and they grew up in a society that was characterised by a focus on doing things well; being pedantic was a good thing while letting go of things was not. This approach is less valued in today's labour market and those who still apply it are getting stressed.

There are exceptions: Some professional groups have always been confronted with an abundance of information and things to do: politicians, lawyers, managing directors, etc., and it appears, based on the interviews with baby boomers, these groups find it easier to deal with the emerging society of information overload.

MORE INFORMATION AVAILABLE—IS THAT REALLY A PROBLEM?

Some sociologists have suggested that a larger amount of information in society leads to a lack of profound knowledge, and the concept of information overload is described in negative terms (e.g., Himma, 2007). Based on a static view of information, it is argued that the more information exists in a society, the more specialised individuals have to be in order to be able to deal with the increasing amount of information (cf. Bush, 1945; Lyttkens, 1988, 1991). And Bush was right when he foresaw a development where it will not be possible to manage all information we collect in our "bewildering store of knowledge" (Bush, 1945). More recently, beginning in the late 1980s, many researchers have developed and conceptualised methods for processing large amounts of information and extracting knowledge, a field of research called Knowledge Management (see, e.g., Alavi & Leidner, 2001; Davenport, De Long, & Beers, 1998; Fuller, 2001; Helleloid & Simonin, 1994; Nonaka & Takeuchi, 1995; Zentes, 1991). Other authors have focused on the severe problems that might be associated with an abundance of information available. Himma is one of many researchers dealing with the increasing amount of information available in society, and more specifically *information overload.*

> Being overloaded with information has undesirable effects on human wellbeing. It diminishes, rather than enhances our well-being and hence can fairly be characterised as 'harming' us. . . . There are, as we will presently see, a variety of deleterious effects of information overload on human wellbeing, but all of them are grounded in the fact that our principal resource for consciously dealing with any problem is a limited one—namely, attention. We cannot consciously address any problem without devoting our conscious focus to it, and we have only so much of this resource available to us. At bottom, then, the information overload problem arises because this cognitive resource is scarce and is being stretched in ways that exceed its limits. (Himma, 2007, p. 267)

Another researcher that deals with individuals' strategies to process information is Thorngate (1988).

> [T]here is no evidence that the rate at which a member of our species can spend attentional resources has increased to any significant degree in the past 10,000 years. As a result, competition for our limited attention has grown in direct proportion to the amount of information available. Because information has been proliferating at such an enormous rate, we have reached the point where attention is an extremely scarce resource. . . . No longer can we believe that information is always an asset, that seeking or consuming it is preferable to ignorance. (Thorngate, 1988, p. 248)

These authors share the idea that we have too much information relative to the scarce attentional resources that can be devoted to processing the information, thus, the information cannot be processed. This situation may be harmful. Thorngate believes that attentional resources cannot be increased, thus neither improved information processing tools nor developed skills will reduce the overload problem.

The perspective in many sociologists', psychologists' and information scientists' research on individuals' information processing seems clear: Ideally, every relevant piece of information should be considered as it might improve the quality of decision making, and too much information makes individuals stressed. As put by Himma (2007):

> But the relevant idea here is that we are aware there is more content out there than we can invest attention in and this causes us psychological discomfort in the form of a host of conditions typically associated with stress: depression, anxiety, a sense of being overwhelmed, and, in extreme cases, panic. (Himma, 2007, p. 268)

Like some other psychologists, Himma emphasises the harmful effect of too much information. This might not be solved through computer-based solutions but rather be experienced by individuals as "technostress" (cf. Brod, 1984; Himma, 2007). Not only for individuals is the abundance of information seen as a problem. Industrial enterprises are reported to find information overload as a serious problem (Öhgren & Sandkuhl, 2008).

BUT WHAT ABOUT INFORMATION OVERLOAD IN THE GENERATION Y SOCIETY?

It appears that the perspective described above does not really apply in the emerging society of Generation Y. For a Generation Y individual, having more content than one can attend to without anxiety and other undesirable psychological effects, as Himma (2007) puts it, appears to be the rule rather than the exception. For individuals who grew up in a society with little information and an opportunity to attend to the existing information (one was aware of) in making decisions, the transition to today's information overloaded society might have been very stressful. But for a Generation Y individual, having an abundance of easily accessible information is the rule, therefore, this does not appear to stress them nearly as much as earlier generations. Figure 2.1 suggests that only 2.8% of Generation Y individuals would prefer to have fewer choices, which is a strong indication that they are not being stressed by having an abundance of information.

To a large extent, the discussion on the abundance of information in society and the problems it entails in terms of information overload and different types of stress appears to *assume that individuals and organisations are expected to make rational, informed decisions* about just about anything that matters. However, in today's society with an abundance of information, a tough business climate, stiff competition in many industries (including the public sector) and a pronounced need of being flexible, customer-oriented and profitable, fully informed decisions appear to be neither possible nor desirable considering their consequences. Generation Y came of age in this society and to them, a new set of values influence the way they approach information.

Consider the early baby boomer couple in the last section on the theme "From lack of information to information overload". They investigate every opportunity and take every piece of information into account before making a decision if it is possible, since they apply the old way of thinking that dominated society during most of their lives and during the grow-up and coming-of-age years particularly. But a Generation Y individual does not strive for making optimal decisions in the old way but rather to make fast, informed and good decisions, which are satisfactory rather than optimal.

As early as 1945, the psychologist Herbert Simon emphasised the cognitive limitations of real minds as opposed to the conceptions of classical rationality, an insight that gave rise to the influential concept of *bounded rationality*. This concept suggests that in decision making, rationality of individuals is limited by the information they have, the cognitive limitations of their minds, and the finite amount of time they have to make decisions. The underlying insight is that the minds of living systems should be interpreted in relation to the environment in which they evolved, rather than to the tenets of classical rationality (Gigerenzer & Goldstein, 2006; see also Simon, 1945, 1956, 1982, 1990). Simon early suggested an alternative basis for the dominating perspective of *rationality as optimisation* in decision making, which views decision making as a fully rational process of finding an optimal choice given the information available (Gigerenzer & Reinhard, 2001).

Another way to look at bounded rationality is that decision makers lack the ability and resources to arrive at the optimal solution, thus they instead apply their rationality only after having greatly simplified the choices available. Hence, the decision maker strives for making satisfactory, not optimal, decisions (cf. Elster, 1983). Already in the 1940s, when the first baby boomers were born, these ideas gained solid ground in some streams of research, although the classical conception of rationality continued to dominate the scene. To Generation Y individuals, fully informed decisions based on the classical notion of reality is the exception. Most decisions that are being made are based on a mixture of intuition and investigation, of emotions and reason, of experiences and expectations, and of one's own conviction and input from others. The process of gathering information and making decisions takes place in a society of a multitude of information sources and channels and a more vague conception about who is an authority.

Experts have always been in power and are likely to keep that position also in the future. However, while experts have traditionally been people with a formal position and many years of experience, an authority may take on many forms, an anonymous user in a web forum, a blogger or an expert from another field (e.g., a former foreign minister commenting a football game or a sitcom star commenting on politics).

To conclude, it is crucial to understand how Generation Y relates to information and decision making to *avoid the common mistake to misinterpret what the other generation is saying and doing*. Having the choice of

100 television channels, 80 secondary schools and companies that supply a product, may it be an insurance, a credit card, electricity or a travel agency service, does not necessarily stress them.

Generation Y individuals know that they are not making optimal decisions in the old sense, and they *distinguish between decisions that are important (or strategic) and those decisions of limited importance*, the latter being, e.g., the choice of electricity supplier or insurance company. Decisions that really matter are, e.g., choice of place to live, people to socialise with, employer, and to an extent, lifestyle consumption. Drawing a parallel to consumer marketing, which discusses high-involvement and low-involvement products (Holmes & Crocker, 1987; Richins & Bloch, 1986; Rotschild, 1979), the similar distinction may be made in decision making. Generation Y individuals put little effort, emotions and time into *low-involvement decisions*, e.g., the choice of electricity or home insurance supplier, but a lot of effort, energy and emotions into *high-involvement decisions*. That being said does not mean the former are not important, but from an overall life perspective, they appear to be less important than the latter. And Generation Y wants to maximise the opportunities that they have in life, which gives little room to engage heavily in every single issue. Marketers and employers should be aware of this transition in attitudes (see Chapter 6).

The next chapter will deal with the emerging market communication landscape and its implications for how Generation Y individuals navigate through today's markets and society. But before that, we will discuss one theme that distinguishes Generation Y from earlier generations—how information is approached, processed and used.

INTERNET—A RELIABLE SOURCE OF INFORMATION?

While many institutions in society—schools, politicians, public authorities, etc.—are bothered by the extensive use of the Internet as an information source, among young people particularly, the Internet is gradually taking over as a reliable source of information. There are certainly flaws in systems like Wikipedia and the validity cannot be guaranteed unless the supplier of the information is well-known. However, the development of the Internet in the last decade or so makes it inconvenient to refuse the Internet as an information source. Firstly, many websites are owned and managed by trustworthy sources, and they published the same material, or at least material that is undergoing similar quality control, in other, offline channels. The websites of British Telecom, The Swedish Embassy in Washington, General Motors and L'Oreal are as reliable as any other information provided by these organisations. Second, the Internet is a fast and transparent medium with many attentive and engaged users. Thus, it is more likely that Siemens or KLM get feedback on faulty online information than on faulty information in offline material, e.g., a brochure on microwave ovens. It is also a lot easier to change the information online compared to asking dealers to send brochures back. Third, the Internet is subject to market forces. If a website provides structured, qualified and easily searchable information, it is likely to have and get many users, thus making it the preferred choice by many users in the category. Poor websites get few users and may have to close down. Fourth, even in cases of open source web pages for which accuracy cannot be guaranteed, e.g., Wikipedia, the quality is surprisingly good. A number of studies confirm the quality of Wikipedia—if you are not convinced, try "colour", "second World War", "Sydney Opera House", "Barack Obama", "Toyota" or "social sciences"! The British journal *Nature* compared Wikipedia to a number of established, printed encyclopedia and found that differences in quality were minor or non-existing. In the study, experts compared 42 articles in Wikipedia and traditional encyclopedia without knowing the source of each article.

In many everyday situations, as well as in many professional situations, the content of Wikipedia or similar sources is good enough.

There is little doubt that Internet encyclopedia like Wikipedia represent a higher quality than newspapers. The latter are under time and cost pressure and are increasingly (sometimes even explicitly!) using Wikipedia in doing research for articles. At the same time, newspapers sometimes criticise young people for lack of critical thinking. A newspaper is not an interactive channel—readers may complain to the editor but that does not change the information provided. While the offline material is written by one single author (or, sometimes, a few authors), the online material undergoes revision from thousands of critical readers. In a critical article in the Arts and Features section of Sweden's leading newspaper, *Dagens Nyheter*, Italian

---

Box 3.3   Girl Power and the Emergence of a New Generation
of TV Stars, Supermodels and Multistars

Popular culture, an increasingly global phenomenon, constitutes an important element of society which Generation Y grew up and came of age in. The diffusion of television through the emergence of satellite and cable television channels contributed to making dramas, soap operas and sitcoms available to a large audience. Many of the programmes originated from the U.S. Some of the sitcoms that Generation Y watched during their teenage years portray females in a different way compared to programmes that were broadcast one or two decades earlier. One of them is *Seinfeld*. Elaine Benes, from the second *Seinfeld* episode one of the four main characters in the sitcom, immediately takes on a progressive role (without proclaiming Girl Power, as the Spice Girls did a few years later) and leaves the traditional behavioural traits attributes that females had at the time in many other television productions behind.

design furniture brand Kartell was described as "a German mass producer of cheap plastic furniture". However, Kartell is neither German, nor cheap. A check with Wikipedia gives the correct answer: Kartell is an Italian producer of classical design furniture, characterised by using perspex in the manufacturing. It is well-known among qualified designers and exposed, e.g., in the Museum of Modern Art in New York. The more critical newspaper readers are and the higher the quality of Internet information, the higher the expectations on newspaper to deliver on their promise—qualified, structured information and knowledge of great quality. Newspaper readers have many other ways to get information and knowledge today, as opposed to a few decades ago, when the newspaper was the dominating information source for most people in the Western world.

SEX AND THE CITY

There would soon be more of this. *Sex and the City* focuses on four New York City women in their mid-to-late-30s (not surprisingly, they got older during the period from 1998 to 2004 that *Sex and the City* was broadcast), columnist Carrie Bradshaw and her three best friends, Miranda Hobbes, Charlotte York and Samantha Jones. The series examined the lives of big-city professional women in the late 1990s/early 2000s and how changing roles and expectations for women affected the characters, and often depicts discussions about romance and sexuality. The four characters represent progress in women's life options and women's empowerment. Not surprisingly, *Sex and the City* has been criticised from various standpoints, e.g., its focus on individualism, beauty and personal upward mobility, and its glamourisation of sex (cf. Akass & McCabe, 2003; Wigmore, 2008) and it certainly has a metro area bias.

Some researchers suggest that *Sex and the City* represents third-wave feminism, e.g., Akass and McCabe (2003): "In its celebration of the joys—and sorrows—of single life, and its ongoing critique of marriage as women's primary goal" (p. 75). Maglin and Perry (1996) even suggest that "Sexuality, in all its guises, has been a kind of lightning rod for this generation's hopes and discontents (and democratic vision) in the same way that civil rights and Vietnam galvanised [a previous] generation in the 1960s" (p. 16). As *Sex and the City* mirrors third-wave writing on feminism, it also gave its critics some arguments. Critics of third-wave feminism argue that it is not political enough, and that it is a highly individualistic philosophy that generally values personal empowerment over collective activism. Thus, it will hardly foster social change. And some critics argue that it does more damage than good by equating women's sexuality with power. Combining postmodernism and feminism appear to provide challenges (cf. Purvis, 2004). Purvis even raises the question whether third-wave feminism is a subculture of Generation X rather than part of feminism.

Sex and the City made—and still makes, while it is being aired and watched by millions of young females all over the world every week—a contribution to female emancipation, and also to the consumption-oriented society. The series' focus on metropolitan life, female empowerment, 30-plus single life in professional jobs with a high living standard and luxury goods has been a reflection of societal changes during Generation Y's coming-of-age period, and also contributed to moving the emerging society forward and communicate its underlying ideology and ideals to countries and places (city and rural areas as opposed to metropolitan areas) where there was little potential to realise the emerging ideal lifestyle.

Needless to say, many other television programmes influenced young people during the 1980s, 1990s and 2000s. *Sex and the City* is one of the most significant examples of how popular culture influences dominating values in society and thus individuals' values, attitudes and behavioural traits.

MODELLING AND THE EMERGENCE OF SUPERMODELS

In another venue of the popular culture—modelling—vast changes took place during the early 1990s and the transition would have a substantial influence on the popular culture during the 1990s, a crucial time period for the Generation Ys cohort[1].

> From 1990–1993, as their success and global recognition grew, the supermodels became superbrands, able to command exorbitant fees and make extraordinary demands, a phenomenon which culminated in Linda Evangelista's notorious quote to American Vogue: 'We don't wake up for less than $10,000 a day.'

Claudia Schiffer describes the experiences from the early 1990s as dramatic: "After the show the Chanel bodyguards would bring me to my car through the crowds of people. It felt like you were coming off the stage from a rock-star tour." And many of the supermodels applied a rock-star lifestyle:

> The supermodels embodied aspirational living. They dressed in the clothes that they modelled, dated actors, musicians and rock starts, and lived lives that paralleled the glamour of their images in magazines and campaigns. Stories of their diva-ish behaviour—real or imagined— filled gossip columns. (Vogue, British Edition, July 2010)

The transition of modelling and the emergence of supermodels is another facet of the emerging equality among the sexes. It was now okay to be a tough girl with power—and males didn't need to be that macho anymore. The balance among the sexes was obviously starting to change.

The global recession in the early 1990s emphasised the need for a new type of model, which was more realistic and less glamorous. There was a new movement of simplicity and rawness in fashion.

> I was looking for a whole new type of girl and that's how I came across Kate. I put Kate in what I was then launching, the CK world, which was supposed to be downtown cool, and Kate embodied that. I thought she was incredibly sexy, she had this slightly androgynous boy–girl, gay–straight thing, and the whole world looked at her in a different way. It wasn't glamorous but it was very hot and sexy and provocative. (Interview with Michael Kors, Vogue, British Edition, July 2010)

A few years later the economy improved and glamour was back in business.

Not everybody liked the transition with supermodels now in power—an industry earlier controlled by (older) men who in various ways took advantage of their strong power position in relation the young girls. That's what they were called—photographer Peter Lindbergh says "They were intelligent women. Whenever I'd yell 'Hey, girls, come over here', Cindy [Crawford] would say, 'We're women, not girls'. They were powerful." The industry was now to a high extent controlled by aware, intelligent and business-minded young (albeit not as young as they used to be) models. The fact that many of the models were living interesting private lives increased the power of the models. "When Kate started dating Johnny Depp things went crazy. A hack hijacked her birthday party, posing as Kate's friend, but no one knew who it was. Her friends locked him into a lavatory," says an agent.

> I think we pushed the editors and designers to their limits and they got fed up. The models' behaviour was borderline insulting—they thought they were invincible and their demands were getting higher and higher. They were commanding everything, the start time, the location. Editors felt manipulated. And they were getting bigger than the designers, who didn't like how the press were only talking about which model went first, and who closed the show. (Interview with Didier Fernandez, Vogue, British Edition, July 2010)

This was still many years before advances in digital technology facilitated a trend for manipulated beauty in fashion imagery, whereby lines were smoothed and defects were banished. That would take off around the start of the new millennium and to an extent bring modelling back to a situation with agencies looking for "the perfect look". This change reduced the room for, and influence of, supermodels with a look or off-stage, private life profile that differentiated her from the norm.

Digital retouching, like cosmetic surgery, meant the industry gravitated towards an ideal beauty, a standard: an almond-shaped face, slim limbs, high eyebrows. Because you could perfect a model's look, and deal with any defects, it gave rise to a homogenised beauty, which in turn became a self-fulfilling prophecy: you had casting agents looking for the girls that looked like the retouched images. (Interview with Robin Derrick, Vogue, British Edition, July 2010)

New technology—in digital retouching and in surgery—gives rise to new behaviours, and people born in the late 1980s may be under stronger influence from these ideals than people born in the early 1980s.

DIVERSITY OF CELEBRITIES AND CHANGING FACETS OF SUPERMODELS

The supermodel is not dead. Just like industry boundaries are changing and becoming increasingly blurred in consumer markets—insurance companies enter the bank business, food retailers deliver parcels earlier provided by the local post office, and gas stations run cafés—modelling now may be part of a superstar's portfolio of activities. Beyoncé, born in 1981, started her career early but became a celebrity during the Destiny's Child girl group years from 1993 to 2001. She began her acting career in 2001 when she appeared in the musical film "Carmen: A Hip Hopera". Hitherto she has worked and reached success as solo music performer, group music performer, singer, songwriter, record producer, actress, dancer, choreographer and video director. Her record sales have surpassed 130 million and she has won several awards (for an updated list, see . . . Wikipedia!). Obviously, the combination of talent, courage and the opportunities that the emerging society offers mentally (it's great to have many occupations!) and through the status of being a celebrity with a strong personal brand.

So there are new ways of becoming a model, and modelling may generate other jobs, reflecting an increasing diversity and the status of being a celebrity as a basis of building a portfolio of competences, occupations, experiences and income sources. Natalia Vodianova emerged as a star in 2003 and quickly cemented a career with big-brand ad campaigns and beauty contracts, Didier Fernandez says "Natalia is a star, she's clever and you have to have a brain to make a career out of fashion. One week she'll work with Anna Wintour, speaking at a model health conference, the next she'll be calling up an artist to get a picture for her charity auction. I can't think of many other models of that generation being that involved" (*Vogue*, 2010).

Hollywood appears to have gotten stronger again. Hollywood stars started replacing models in the late 1990s, shooting cover stories and being awarded beauty contracts and advertising campaigns. Alexandra

Shulman says "The backlash against the supermodels led to designers looking for endorsement from new faces. They turned to Hollywood, where a new generation of stars—Gwyneth Paltrow, Sarah Jessica Parker, Jennifer Lopez—were interested in fashion and glamour, and prepared to be styled and photographed" (*Vogue*, 2010). Sarah Jessica Parker already had an aura of glamour at the time through her role as Carrie Bradshaw in *Sex and the City*. Later, Emma Watson, Blake Lively and numerous male models[2] entered the scene as actors, and then became more or less involved in modelling.

Celebrities are important marketers for companies who pay large sums to make the right person use their products, and expose the usage in the right context. This is nothing new and is closely related to product placement. A practice that has turned more common is to involve celebrities as more formal spokespersons or in the board of directors. This underlines the good chances in today's society for people who became famous for one thing they did to use this as a venue for getting access to another area of art, competence or expertise. For instance, Earth Biofuels, Inc., a U.S. company that produces, supplies and distributes of alternative based fuels, i.e., biodiesel, ethanol and liquid natural gas, has engaged numerous celebrities. Julia Roberts, Morgan Freeman, music legend Willie Nelson and NASCAR-driver Rusty Wallace have joined the company's Advisory Board and they also act as spokespersons for the company, thus promoting the use of renewable fuels. This practice may cause problems since spokespeople may misuse their reputation by speaking for something as part of a remunerated lobbying rather than expressing their genuine thoughts and values.

HOW ARE CHANGES COMING ABOUT?

The conclusion from the previous description of the development is that people want content—and a superstar with a life that people know about gives the model a context and makes her more real. "Actresses have been taking over the covers of magazines and advertising campaigns because people want content. They want to know who the girl on the cover has dated, what parties she's been to, what outfits she wore. When you do a cover with an actress, the reader is not looking at the dress she's wearing, they're looking at her whole lifestyle" (*Vogue*, 2010). Even magazines issued every week have recent pictures of celebrities on parties and grade the dresses they wear—sometimes readers are invited to vote). The great exposition of the looks and lifestyle of celebrities is also a strong reason for marketers to work with models, supermodels, multistars or just celebrities or whatever they might be called. The percentage of Generation Y individuals who state that they are influenced by the social environment, meaning friends and global celebrities, both are a lot higher than for baby boomers, particularly the influence from global celebrities.

Along with this development, the number of magazines about stars exploded and paparazzi found an increasing number of channels for their photographs.

But how do these changes come about? A complex set of factors in the macro environment in combination with specific events that are difficult to forecast, e.g., the coming together of two people. The soil in which British supermodels emerged is suggested to have been driven by the optimism that a new political scene created.

> Led by a young Tony Blair, Labour won the general election on a plat-form of modernisation in 1997, and the country experienced a ground-swell of optimism. Along with Britpop bands and YBAs, young British designers like Alexander McQueen and Husseing Chalayan gave rise to the 'Cool Britannia' moment. In 1997 Karen Elson became fashion's new it-girl after being persuaded by Steven Meisel to chop her hair off, dye it red and shave her eyebrows. Suddenly, quirky-looking British models were in high demand. (Vogue, 2010)

This is one of many possible explanations. Like many other historical events, there are different ways of describing how they came about. But the conclusion must be that companies need to constantly watch the environ-ment and also stay in touch with popular culture and new trends—but this need varies with customer profile and product. To a high extent, the success of Swedish beverage company Spendrups is explained by the company being in touch with popular culture (see case on Spendrups in Kotler et al., 2011)

> Look, there is my best guy, he knows exactly what is happening in Stockholm's night life. And that's where all the new marketing begins. I'm too old for understanding these things know—and I can't under-stand why people buy beer with a skull on the label—but it sells. So I need him and the other young guys. (Ulf Spendrup, baby boomer and vice president, Spendrups Brewery, in an interview when a red Porsche showed up at the company park slot)

THE WORLD IS CLOSER AND MORE TRANSPARENT— AN OPPORTUNITY FOR TALENTS WITHOUT NETWORKS, MONEY AND CELEBRITY PARENTS

The multitude of television programmes with a strong reality connec-tion—*Idol* (*American Idol*/*Britain's Got Talent*, etc.), *Big Brother*, *The Apprentice*, *Project Runaway*, to mention a few that are aired all over the world—transfers a message to young watchers, with their frame of refer-ences founded in the emerging society of Generation Y and beyond: You can be what you want, just take the chances you are given! This is a tough world for many people and the pressure on young people to profile themselves, develop their talents and stay competitive is by many individuals experienced as severe. Particularly in countries like China, where young people are subject to the six-pocket syndrome, meaning that the often only kid in the family has six parents (parents and grandparents) that put pressure on her or him to perform well, the pressure is severe. And this causes a lot of stress on individuals. If earlier stress was caused by people not having the time to go through every piece of information and a fear of not living up to high expectations on performance of individual tasks (see earlier in the chapter), pressure now comes from the frustration caused by the fact that individuals cannot be what they want. The world around them says: Take every opportunity! Study two university programmes! Learn more languages! Television and other channels represent an overflow of people who succeeded, beautifully designed apartments, glamorous and nice pieces of clothing, etc.

If earlier—at the time baby boomers came of age—the influences on young peoples' thought about career, education, etc., were restricted to the family, friends and to a limited extent the few mass communication channels that existed, influences now come from many sources—a multitude of television programmes and websites, celebrities and multistars (which now are scrutinised more closely), social networks, mass media, etc. The sources of influence have become more global. And, as we will see in Chapter 5, influence is also strong from friends, colleagues and other elements in the social environment that contribute to the pressure.

Television programmes bring the world closer to the individuals who watch the television and with a reality-based content, like *Idol* and the other television formats suggested above, television may provide opportunities for unknown individuals, with few opportunities provided through parents, family contacts or financial wealth, to become stars. A pattern that may be identified in most countries is that those who succeed in reality television programmes often come from a middle-class or working-class background, which most likely mirrors the profile of those who apply.

Even though relatively few people succeed, the reality television programmes obviously provide hope and inspiration to people—thousands of people apply in each country where *American Idol/Britain's Got Talent* and other spin-offs of the British *Pop Idol* (which has become a successful international franchise!) run. Some seasons there have been more than 100,000 people auditing for *American Idol*. This type of opportunity— and also risk of being exposed in a poor way—mirrors and contributes to the society that Generation Y comes of age in. The old wisdom suggested money, contacts and talent to succeed—the new wisdom suggests courage, the right attitude (don't give up—there will always be more opportunities!) and talent. And the opportunities provided through new technology—e.g., Internet channels such as MySpace.com (2003) and YouTube.com (2005)— have contributed to this important change.

EMPIRE BUILDING OR ENJOYING LIFE?

A pattern that emerges in analysing the Generation Y cohort is the lower propensity to engage in empire building—and, which needs some further comments, a higher propensity to maximise current opportunities and enjoy life. The former is more clear than the latter, since earlier generations are increasingly engaging in self-realisation and life enjoyment when opportunities to do so arise financially and practically. However, for baby boomers life enjoyment may be inconsistent with the set of values they grew up with, and is not as natural as for Generation Y individuals.

For baby boomers, the strong tendency to build empires may be derived from the values that characterised their growing up and coming-of-age years. Strong values at the time (cf. Meredith, Schewe, Hiam, & Karlovich, 2002; Meredith, Schewe, & Karlovich, 2002; Parment, 2009c, 2011; Schewe & Meredith, 2004; Meredith & Schewe, 1984) built on the following principles:

- *Saving money for the future.* After World War II insecurity about the future was a value that characterised peoples' lives. Societal institutions, employers, banks, politics—many crucial elements of a stable, growth-oriented economy had been absent for many years. Thus, saving for a rainy day was seen as necessary and individuals could not trust politics or employers to provide for their futures. Those values were born by baby boomers and generations before them throughout the extensive growth period in the 1950s and 1960s.
- *Not borrowing more money than is necessary.* It was seen as irresponsible to borrow money for consumption that was anything but necessary for survival. No one would come up with the idea to take a loan to go on vacation with the family, and few families would replace the kitchen for aesthetic reasons only (which is rather common today, particularly in metropolitan areas). Financing a house through bank loans might have been necessary, but the plan was normally to pay off the loans in 20 or 30 years time, something Generation Y individuals neither can nor want to do given the house and apartment prices in today's markets.
- *Building up something that lasts.* It was seen as reasonable and fair to leave more to the next generation than one inherited from parents and grandparents. Many decisions and behavioural traits were built around continuity, stability and building up for the future: Collections of year books, encyclopedias, recipes and magazines were stored; notes from lectures, meetings and conferences were, like photographs and many other things, organised, compiled and indexed. Automobiles, grass mowers and leather upholstery sofas were cleaned and inspected according to manufacturer recommendations, to last longer and maintain resale values. Inspection guidelines had authority,

people had the time to care about maintaining their belongings and it was even seen as a shame not to look after one's belongings. Products were bought for their functions rather than emotions, lifestyle, image or latest design, which reflect more limited financial resources. There were few if any manufacturer warranties and consumer rights so it was very much up to the owner to look after goods to make sure they lasted for a long time. Not only consumption patterns and style (a concept hardly used at the time) but also career planning (one-firm commitment, often staying in the same industry and type of company) and residence planning (the concept of "residence career" did not exist—at least not in its more recent, speculative sense) were characterised by gradually building up something that would provide adequate supply in the future.

- *Basing purchase decisions primarily on rational criteria as opposed to emotions* was a natural consequence of limited financial room for extravagances, high prices compared to disposable income of clothing, white goods, cars and many other items, less supply of emotional products and a societal culture with reason rather than emotions and self-fulfillment as dominant discourse. The consumption culture gave little room for emotions with the exception of the youth consumption culture and some subcultures that the mass market did not engage in. The dominating collectivistic values (as opposed to today's strong emphasis on individualism) suggested an emphasis on reason and general emerging "needs" for automobiles, washing machines and freezers (all very expensive and energy-inefficient at the time) certainly provided image and self-fulfillment to the proud owner, but was often bought for the products' functionality in the first place.

More recently, baby boomers have gradually become more open to emotional, experience-based consumption, but still bear the old values in mind when making purchase decisions. This is obvious in purchase situations, where they are attracted by emotional products but, because of the values that guide them and the way they discuss decisions they make, do not realise themselves. Out of 20 interviewed baby boomers, none spontaneously "confessed" to be emotional in her or his purchase decisions. However, one 63-year-old male interviewee, who strongly emphasised that all purchase decisions he made were driven by reason and not emotions, sent an e-mail a few days after the interview. He is a lawyer which most likely influenced the way he formulated the e-mail.

After the interview I've thought a lot about decisions I've made in my life and, with hindsight, I realise that some of the purchase decisions were actually emotional, a few of them may even have been spontaneous impulse purchases based on little research. However, the number and purchase amount of impulse buying is strikingly small compared to the overall purchase volume I represent. Some of the impulse buying even turned out to be good buys.

The way baby boomers argue with regards to choices they make reflect the set of values that characterise their generation. Individuals with very high incomes are no exception. A senior executive living in an upmarket house and, as it appears, consistently buying and using upmarket premium products (Bang & Olufsen audio system, BMW cars, Fritz Hansen chairs, Poggenpohl kitchen, etc.) emphasises that "all purchase decisions are based on functionality in the first place" (female, born 1952). Another baby boomer with average income suggests that he bought his EUR 60,000 BMW "for three reasons: fuel efficiency, high resale value, and 30,000km inspection intervals" (male, born 1951). However, after a discussion on emotions and reason he confessed that he likes the design of the car and that "it might have had an impact on the decision to buy it". The strong tendency to emphasise rational arguments that characterised all 20 interviewed baby boomers was manifested in different ways, e.g., by seeing leisure travel or expensive furniture as an investment.

> I'm not that interested in furniture. We bought a new sofa, the old one was broken, we bought on price . . . the purchase of the carpet maybe had some emotional influence . . . the price was EUR 2,000, but it will last for a lifetime, even though we spill wine and coffee on it . . . the chair here was EUR 1,700, it's nice, you got me, it certainly was an emotional buy to an extent. (male, born 1946)

> Travelling is an investment and it contributes to developing your career, I travelled a lot in Europe and the US, you learn a lot, you increase your understanding of other cultures, things you can't really learn by reading a book. (male, born 1942)

THE END OF THE EMPIRE BUILDING ERA AND THE GRADUAL MOVE AWAY FROM INHERITING CAREERS, STRUCTURES, STYLES AND MANNERS

What is empire building then? It is about building, saving, planning and striving for ownership rather than enjoying, and taking things as they come. For instance, a few baby boomers proudly accounted for how they amortised mortgages and built an additional house in the summer cottage—"to make room for the grandchildren". They expect the children and grandchildren to want to stay there, and they want to leave something to the next generation. What is the problem with such an approach? Nothing from the baby boomer perspective, and many children and grandchildren are happy to have a place where they can meet their family on a regular basis. As we will see in Chapter 5, Generation Y in general terms have good relations with their parents. However, Generation Y individuals may not want to take over and organise summer cottages, organise big family parties, inherit living places, family companies, etc., from their parents. Empire building—maintaining and developing something that parents inherited or built up—is not the main focus of Generation Y. If they want to move, they will do that. If they want to stay somewhere else during the summertime, they are likely to be doing that. And if they inherit something from their parents that they do not want, they are likely to say that instead of inheriting and getting another burden upon their shoulders.

How did this development come about? More ideas, a broader frame of references and a changed view on authorities give Generation Y individuals the courage not to take over living patterns and manners from parents. This transition has been going on for many decades, and maybe even centuries. A century back or more, individuals married to survive—often with locals or friends of the family. Visiting an adjacent town to see somebody was seen as intruding from the other town's perspective. Few people moved or attended higher education. Visiting the country capital was a seldom exception and travelling abroad (a very expensive venture at the time) was something for rich and famous people. Most people took over the parents' family business if they had one, or inherited the profession from their parents. Most females worked at home, many hours a day. Self-realisation was nothing to think about as a daily enjoyment.

Then, gradually, self-realisation and doing something parents did not became more common. This development started earlier in countries like the U.S. which enjoyed substantial economic growth and also a culture where people moved more regularly already in the first decades of the 20th century, before the Great Depression. In many developed countries, it was not until after World War II that the development towards today's society of self-realisation started. High economic growth, a substantial increase in the number of higher education students, and the emergence of a youth culture (which in turn was made possible by radio, television, LP records and a changed attitude) made the 1950s and 1960s crucial in understanding the development towards today's situation[3]. In the post WWII era people realised many opportunities that hardly existed before but, as we will see, with a mindset that differed from that of Generation Y.

Gradually, as the financial situation has become better and as children have moved out and, as one reaches the end of the career, employer and labour market pressure loosens, it is becoming practically feasible to do what many people, regardless of their generational cohort belonging, like: Enjoy life, travel, dining out, etc. The major difference is that for baby boomers, it does not come naturally: Many of them are strongly influenced by the values they have born since their childhood, meaning they don't prioritise free time and they don't even want it. For young people, self-realisation and daily life enjoyment is something natural that became an integrated part of their mindsets during their coming-of-age years.

A BRANDED SOCIETY: THE DISAPPEARANCE OF NON-COMMERCIAL ZONES

Still in the 1970s and 1980s, many environments that individuals got in contact with on a daily basis were free from commercial messages: They were non-commercial zones. Gradually, these environments disappeared and became replaced by an ideology that gained solid ground during the 1980s particularly. The 1980s, the decade of Reaganomics and Thatcherism, showed an emergence of strong preferences for the small state and free markets (cf. Bienkowski, Brada, & Radlo, 2006; Jenkins, 2006; Niskanen, 1988; Pratten, 1997; Skidelsky, 1988; Vinen, 2009; Wood, 1991), privatisation (cf. the literature on New Public Management, e.g., Ferlie et al., 1996; Hood, 1995) and individualism (Freeman & Bordia, 2001; Triandis, 1993; see also Schimmack, Oishi, & Diener, 2005). The interest for brands took off on a broader basis, and not only were for-profit businesses running brand management programmes: Also, NGOs, cities, employers and societal institutions discovered the benefits of profiling the brand in an increasingly competitive environment and a market communication landscape with an ever increasing number of commercial messages.

Generation Y grew up in the emerging branded society and see branding efforts of municipalities, public transport services, churches and, which has been emphasised more lately, individuals (often referred to as Personal Branding, see, e.g., Goldsmith et al., 2009; Purkiss & Royston-Lee, 2009; Spillane, 2000; Wilson & Blumenthal, 2008; Vickers et al., 2008) as something natural.

Canadian author and sociologist Naomi Klein presented many thoughts on our branded society in her influential bestseller *No Logo: Taking Aim at the Brand Bullies*, which was launched in year 2000. Being a critical author, Klein describes the negative effects of brand-oriented activities and also methods individuals and movements have used to fight back against companies that use their brand power in an unfair way.

Klein argues that there has been a shift in the usage of branding, from putting a recognisable face on factory-produced products—at the time multinational corporations had limited market power—to the idea of selling lifestyles and, since the 1980s, a new era with brand names and logos beginning to appear everywhere. Klein describes how brands like Nike and Pepsi attempt to have their names associated with everything from movie stars and athletes to grassroots social movements. The brand name gradually has become more important than the actual product, according to Klein. Interestingly, Klein discusses how many consumer brands work

hard to gain presence into the school system, and thus getting brand exposition and feedback back from the students. The effects are fewer choices
through the strong market dominance of retail chains (Hennes & Mauritz, McDonald's, Wal-Mart) or manufacturer-owned stores. Klein also
discusses the structural change from local manufacturing to production
in export processing zones, places where few or no labour laws exist but
manufacturing costs are very low.

Klein's perspective is interesting since it deals with structural changes
in society that, e.g., business students hardly hear of while attending business schools, at least not in the critical or negative way. One of the many
corporate practices described by Klein—university campuses where only
one brand in a particular category is being sold—has been a lot more common since the *No Logo* book was written. And in the last decades society
has undergone a development towards branding of just about everything—
students associations, university campuses and educational programmes.
And, students are targets of many branding activities: Employers brand
themselves to attract the right students, and school cafes and restaurants,
earlier owned and run by the school, have gradually been taken over by
domestic and international food retail chains.

As with other phenomena described in this book, the perspective, expectations and tolerance of the brand dimension of society is different for
Generation Y, individuals who grew up in a society that largely resembles
today's society, although many practices have become more pronounced in
the last decade.

THE DISAPPEARANCE OF A CLEAR DIVISION
BETWEEN WORK AND LEISURE TIME

Once upon a time, and as a dominating principle in many countries and
contexts until the 1960s or 1970s, society was organised based on a
clear division between work and leisure time. With few exceptions, people worked from the early morning to the late afternoon, and leisure time
activities were available during weekends, public holidays and to an extent
on weekday nights. Stores closed at 5, 6 or 7 p.m. and public transport
brought workers to the workplace at a time that fitted with the working
hours. Individuals had little choice but to follow the rhythm. Television was
available during a few hours on weekday nights and during weekends, and
there were few channels to choose between. No coworker would come up
with the idea to ask for starting at 9 a.m. instead of 6:30 and bus companies were hardly asked to run buses at odd hours to reflect individual travel-
lers' demands for their own rhythm and self-realisation. Society provided a
rhythm and citizens, with some but few exceptions, followed it. Gradually,
this society has been replaced by a 24/7 society.

THE EMERGENCE OF A SERVICE-DOMINANT LOGIC

Not only has the share of services increased, the focus on physical products has also been replaced by a *service-dominant logic*, meaning that also in traditional, goods-based industries, the logic of services is taking over (Lusch, Vargo, & O'Brien, 2007; Vargo & Lusch, 2004a, 2004b). As suggested by Vargo and Lusch (2004a), this approach emphasises that both service companies and goods companies are producing services: Something that is solving a problem or satisfying the need for a customer; people buy goods because they want services. For instance, a sports car transfers a number of services to the user, the mixture of which depends on buyer characteristics and the situation at hand—showing off, satisfying a need for independence, preference for dynamic and sporty products, enjoying the driving experience; displaying high income, etc. That being said, there are most likely other products that individually or in combination with more products can contribute to the services that the sports car (or other product at hand) conveys.

Generation Y individuals are used to the attitudes that the reorientation towards market forces, many consumer choices, increased competition and a service-dominant logic have created. To them, the traditional distinction between goods and services makes sense, but is far from as clear as it is for individuals born in the 1930s, 1940s, 1950s and 1960s, who came of age in a society that distinguished clearly between tangible goods and perishable, intangible, heterogenous and—not explicitly said but understood—less reliable services. Over time, companies have put a lot of effort into standardising and controlling services, which has made them more product-like: The quality has increased while the variation between retailers, restaurants, sites or employees has diminished. As put by a car manufacturer CEO (quoted in Parment, 2009a):

> From the customer's point of view, one of the key points in retailing is to always dream of this as a factory, to have standard processes. So when the customer goes to a dealership, any dealership, they get handled properly, every time.

Although this is likely to be a dream rather than practice—there will certainly be variations across dealers and people buying from people means deviations from a standardised process—it manifests an attitude that reflects the strong tendency in retailing to standardise and deliver on the ambitious brand and customer promises most companies now have. Generation Y individuals are used to customer promises, a high level of consumer rights, and channels for customer complaints. They don't apply the old wisdom of rich companies that do what they can to exploit poor consumers, but rather a more balanced perspective with aware and knowledgeable consumers dealing with companies that certainly are profit-oriented, but with high ambitions to strengthen their brands by delivering on their promises. Grassroots criticism and feedback contributes to putting pressure on companies to behave well.

We will now look at the market environment, where the societal changes dealt with in this chapter are manifested.

4 Generation Y and the Market Environment

Chapter 4 describes the market environment and how competitive mechanisms influence supply and demand patterns. Changes in the last decades in market environments are analysed, e.g., changes in state regulation, the emergence and growth of free trade, the increased supply of low-cost production and the emergence of a multitude of brands, which gives consumers many choices. Consistency in branding and policies are discussed as well as competitive advantages—something every business with ambitions to compete in today's market environment needs to consider.

Many of these changes embrace labour markets alike, and in companies' attempts to create and develop competitiveness, coworkers are crucial. In the emerging market environment, coworkers have a crucial role, something that is considered in this chapter.

The market environment is a key element in any analysis of marketing in general and more specifically consumer behaviour. The market environment makes room for consumer behaviour but may also put restrictions on individuals' choices and opportunities in the marketplace.

This chapter will examine some major trends and forces that are changing the market environment landscape and in turn provide a challenge for companies in designing marketing strategy. We look at four important developments that have an influence on the market environment—the information revolution, Globalisation, the call for more ethics and social responsibility, and the expanding reach and scope of marketing. Needless to say, there are many more to discuss and the list might be much lengthier.

THE INFORMATION REVOLUTION

The information revolution has been going on for several decades, but accelerated in the last decade. It is mainly technology-driven: Advances in computer, communications, information, and other digital technologies have had a major impact on the ways individuals and companies gather information and communicate. The changes mean that marketers can no longer expect consumers to always seek them out. Nor can they always control conversations about their brands. Marketing content and pictures as well as criticism and complaints are now easily available on the Internet. Even though many businesses are highly aware of this, the consequences are often not fully understood and the Generation Y cohort will more than any generation before make use of the new opportunities that arise—an opportunity or a threat to companies depending on how they approach Generation Y individuals and whether their talents are made use of.

The changes and opportunities that come with the information revolution have created a different set of attitudes and traits among consumers. Thanks to the Internet, consumer power has got stronger: There is now a multitude of opportunities to get informed about what peers say about a furniture store, a piece of clothing, a car, a restaurant, an airline, a hotel, a business school, an employer or even a doctor or a teacher.

The emerging customer-oriented and consumer power driven market environment now also embraces the labour market, where grassroots driven information has become increasingly difficult. What this change means for the labour market is illustrated in the case on Glassdoor (see Chapter 6), by Facebook groups that deal with individual coworkers' relations with and experiences with employers, and Internet forums where matters related to the labour market are discussed.

It is hard to find a company that doesn't use the Web in a significant way. Most traditional "brick-and-mortar" companies have now become "click-and-mortar" companies. Some companies provide user's guides and software also for 10-year-old products on their websites—a great opportunity to stay attractive among consumers who have a problem solved easily through visiting the website. A SonyEricsson user may wonder where the drivers for the mobile phone–computer interface are. A visit at sonyericsson.com starts with an offer on software updates, and by scrolling down the user gets direct links to the user's guide, software and troubleshooting. For Generation Y, it is natural to use these tools and they no longer see traditional dichotomies such as between goods and services as important.

MORE ETHICS AND SOCIAL RESPONSIBILITY

As the worldwide consumerism and environmentalism—both critical towards the consumption-oriented society—mature, companies are being called upon to take greater responsibility for the social and environmental impact of their actions. The consumerism (cf. Bell & Emory, 1971; Barksdale & Darden, 1972; Buskirk & Rothe, 1970; Kangun, Cox, Higginbotham, & Burton, 1975; Kotler, 1972) and environmentalism (cf. Banerjee, Lyer, & Kashyap, 2003) movements took off in the early 1970s and contributed to a significant pressure on companies to take a broader perspective on marketing. The message of these movements were clear: Not only consumer tastes and preferences need to be considered but also the effect of consumption on society and other stakeholders. There have been some influential initiatives also later, e.g., Naomi Klein's *No Logo* (2001)[1], which provides a criticism on global corporations particularly and how they explore opportunities to manufacture at low cost, emphasise branding heavily and then overmarket the products to consumers in rich countries.

In the last few years, corporate ethics and social responsibility have become hot topics for almost every business. And few companies can ignore the renewed and very demanding environmental movement. Every company action can affect its relationships with customers.[2]

GLOBALISATION AND INTERNATIONALISATION

Globalisation and Internationalisation—two inherently distinctive but highly related concepts—are crucial to understand the changes society and consumer markets have undergone in the last few decades. Globalisation has many facets, meanings and implications—political, demographic, economic, cultural and ecological—and the Globalisation forces that have been in place in the last decades have created markets that are inherently different from what they were before. Consumers throughout the Western world have access to cheap furniture, clothing and consumer electronics for a fraction of the (inflation-adjusted) prices charged a few decades ago. The awareness and knowledge about other cultures have increased through extensive— and much cheaper—travel, and individuals in all developed countries have imported and integrated consumption styles from other parts of the world.

As opposed to just one or a few decades ago, almost every company is touched in some way by global competition. Today, companies are not only trying to sell more of their locally produced goods in international markets, they also are buying more supplies and components abroad. Small, local companies increasingly compete with big international companies. Neighborhood stores and service providers must deliver consumer value to stay viable, and more so than international chains as the locals often have higher prices, something that may be eliminated by increased competition. Any local service must deliver upon ambitious promises, may it be local, independently run and owned hotels, restaurants or retailers under competition from international chains. As consumers are more well-informed and use the Internet to compare prices, local stores can hardly charge higher prices as they did in the past. A global view of the company's industry, competitors and opportunities is necessary to compete now and in the future.

Cheaper transport is a cornerstone in the substantial increase in international trade. For instance, the emergence and rapid growth of container modules in the 1970s, which made transfer between means of transport easier, radically improved the opportunities of trading across borders, continents and geographical regions. In the 1970s, it took 108 people 5 days to empty a transportation ferry—with containers, the same job is done with eight people in 1 day, a reduction of man hours by 98.5% (Peters, 2000).

In our changing world, a lot may happen in the coming years and Western countries may overestimate the power of Western management and practice, based on an attitude of seeing Western countries as the norm in running an enterprise effectively and efficiently. Emerging countries and companies should not be underestimated. China, India, Mexico and other growing countries (it appears increasingly passé to classify these countries as emerging countries—they have long been established major players in the world business) have a lot of knowledge about Western companies and brands and what is going on in our cultural sphere. They often listen to Western music, and watch Western movies and television. At the same time, Western consumers, investors, business leaders and politicians know very little about countries in other parts of the world, and their major companies and consumption styles.

A few decades ago, the Western world could be comfortable with the situation—there was a steady flow of influences from the Western world to the emerging countries and hardly something the other way round. People outside the Western world liked our brands and with few exceptions, the world wanted our music, our consumption style, our brands and, maybe, our management style. At least they looked upon the Western style, which set the tone in many parts of the world. Even though this still applies to an extent, e.g., with music and other influences from popular culture, it can not be taken for granted that the situation will remain in the future. As the "emerging" countries become more powerful—they actually own an increasing percentage of companies, brands and operations in the Western world—they are likely to be less influenced by the Western world in their consumption styles. We do not really know what will happen in decades to come, but every organisation, and particularly those in major Western countries, should follow the development and be careful not to disregard the power of countries which have not been very powerful in the last decades but now come with an increasing substance of consumption-hungry customers, technological knowledge and enthusiasm to grow and prosper.

COMPETITION IS GETTING MORE GLOBAL

To companies this transition might be a huge opportunity and it is now a lot easier to reach other countries: Mental and trade barriers have been reduced or removed altough, at times, governments in some countries may introduce new barriers. Over time, however, the tendency is clear: World markets are becoming increasingly integrated. For competitive companies, this has meant huge opportunities to build an international reputation—which is easier than before, since consumers are more open-minded and there are more communication vehicles available—and expand into new markets, thus benefiting from economies of scale and brand power.

However, companies that lack competitive power have seen their markets gradually disappear. Consumer loyalty to local stores has diminished and few consumers now want to pay a substantial price premium for buying from a local provider, unless the provider delivers in accordance with what competitors offer. A company can—and this has not changed—charge higher prices or enjoy consumers despite a limited service level or product range if the localisation is advantageous to the consumer. However, few consumers support local businesses automatically, as they did in the past when consumers supported local businesses afraid of seeing them disappear. An opportunity for local businesses with a limited market is to sell on the ecological advantages of buying locally. Consumers are increasingly aware of the holistic effects of buying locally.

The Internet, consumer rights and more critical consumer attitudes towards what companies offer make life tough for companies that do not deliver on consumer expectations and demands. Generation Y has grown up with this emerging set of attitudes and automatically apply a tougher attitude towards companies than earlier generations who have experienced the transition from selling firms being in power to strong consumer rights. Companies must consider the transition in power balance to the consumers' favour. The higher the percentage of aware and critical customers, the more important for companies to be prepared to deal with consumer preferences, expectations and feedback.

While a consumer earlier bought craftsman services from a trusted local provider, consumers are now open for buying the services from an adjacent city, through an Internet agency or from a non-domestic supplier. A car buyer that always trusted the local, authorised repairshop may trust an Internet bidding service to find a lower price. Insurances and bank services may be bought from a trustworthy (which may be confirmed by other Internet users) domestic or non-domestic supplier that delivers on the consumer's preferences at a good price.

INCREASED VALUE OF INTANGIBLES

The trend towards an emphasis on intellectual, artistic and emotional aspects of brands and products has been going on during the entire 20th century and continued in recent years. For Generation Y, these aspects of a product are as natural as the tangible content.

The profession that is now referred to as designer appears to have started with the German architect Peter Behrens when he, around year 1908, began designing almost everything for German producer of electrical equipment AEG, including not only the company's various products but also the factory facilities, fonts, prints, postcards, catalogs and annual reports. Behrens actually gave AEG a consistent graphic profile. Typical of the time was that one single person was responsible for the entire process and kept it completely under his control (Brunnstrom, 2004; Buddensieg et al., 1985; Kadatz, 1977). Behrens laid the foundation for what has increasingly come to be seen as central to being able to communicate clearly and effectively with a market: A clear corporate identity that characterises everything that the organisation does (cf. Birkigt et al., 1992) and as part of its self-image (cf. Salzer, 1994).

In the last decades, cost structures have changed fundamentally. While older people may obviously apply a frame of references that does not longer apply—"Please keep your long-distance calls short, it's so expensive" or "We need to repair the DVD player, it doesn't work" are typical statements of older people, not aware of the fact that long-distance domestic calls are likely to cost the same as calling a neighbour, and a new cheap DVD player costs about EUR 30. These changes are the result of international trade, new manufacturing technologies and manufacturing in low-cost countries. However, services and experiences can not be standardised to as high an extent as can the manufacturing of products. Hence, the increased service content in most products counterbalance the savings created by cheaper manufacturing of goods. White goods, Italian pasta, automobiles, furniture and clothing are all subject to money spent on creating customer experiences, on warranties, living up to generous product return policies, customer magazines and other benefits, that generate customer advantages but increase costs.

From a value chain perspective the changes result in a changed emphasis—if earlier manufacturing costs constituted a major part of the costs generated through the value chain, they now only constitute a smaller part of the product's end price. From a marketing perspective this means a transition from *cost-based pricing* to *value-based pricing* (cf. Kotler et al., 2011). This change has been going on for decades and for the Generation Y cohort, basing pricing decisions on the customer value a product entails is something natural. And customer value is crucial to decisions to buy a product. Accordingly, companies spend an increasing amount of effort and money on creating experiences and emotions in product development and marketing. This practice drives costs and thus makes room for new actors that present a scaled down business model, e.g., RyanAir or IKEA. When existing firms add service after service, afraid of being competitively disadvantaged, there is an increased chance of low-cost actors entering the industry, a tendency described already half a decade ago by Hollander (1960) with the *Wheel of Retailing* theory.

In most countries, goods manufacturing are not the key to societal prosperity and economic growth. And service-intensive geographical areas often do better during a financial crisis than manufacturing-intensive areas.

THE EXPANDING REACH AND SCOPE OF MARKETING

In the past, marketing has been most widely applied in the for-profit business sector and new marketing ideas often emerged from creative marketing departments in big multinational enterprises. Many sectors in society, including not only the public sector but also to extent insurance companies, banks, auditing firms and cultural institutions (for-profit or not), hardly engaged in marketing. Certainly they worked with their *reputation* as a long-term *raison d'entrê* but hardly with specific marketing tools. The competition intensity was limited, since markets were local or domestic, consumers less informed and demanding, and public authorities were not very active in supporting citizens in making clever, well-informed buying decisions.

In recent years, however, marketing also has become a major part of the strategies of many not-for-profit organisations, e.g., universities, schools, hospitals, museums and churches. Not-for-profits face stiff competition for support and membership for a number of reasons. Consumers experience that they have less time than before—at the same time, the number of activities available has increased substantially. Regardless of whether an individual lives in a metropolitan area or a rural area, the age of the individual, confessional belonging and the cultural context—there is an increasing amount of activities that compete on attention and the individuals' time. Most not-for-profit organisations find it more difficult than before to get committed people engaged in their activities. Sound marketing can help them attract membership and support.[3]

Examples of how not-for-profit organisations practice marketing are numerous. An interesting example is Church of Sweden. Not only through the homepage www.svenskakyrkan.se, but also through a Facebook group, both active church members and others interested in the church, Christian faith and how one may help people in great need of social support (e.g., after a Tsunami or major earthquake) and religious guidelines have a platform and source of knowledge. To decrease the threshold for people not used to visiting a church, it is even possible to write a prayer on the Church of Sweden website.

A BROADER SCOPE AND APPLICATIONS OF BRANDS

Cities, regions and individuals have become more active in promoting their brands. Both cities with an inherent attraction, e.g., Barcelona, Beijing, New York, Stockholm and Sydney, and cities that have something to offer but have not really came to the point where the general public is aware of this, work more systematically than ever to promote their brands. Bilbao and Birmingham have been in such a situation with little attractivity among the public in general and despite this developed their city brand positions. Meanwhile, other cities, e.g., Leipzig, have a lot of potential but have not really broken through the media noise. The branding of places goes under many names, e.g., city branding, destination branding and place branding. Like employer branding and personal branding, the inspiration to a high extent comes from consumer branding.

Interestingly, these emerging spheres of marketing and branding are overlapping, and many marketing efforts are made by going beyond the traditional consumer branding scene. For instance, the success of many employer brands are a direct consequence of their strong positions in the consumer markets, e.g., Audi, BMW, BPP Group, Google, Hennes & Mauritz, IKEA and Unilever. Many celebrities like Lady Gaga, Beyoncé, Dr. Phil, Donald Trump and Oprah Winfrey are both very active in promoting their personal brands—although seldom explicitly—and representing the organisations, companies and ventures they work for, and may have ownership of.

One example of this practice of making use of strong brands in different brand spheres—an interpretation of co-branding, a concept originally representing two or more companies doing marketing together in consumer markets—is Oprah Winfrey's show in Australia. Winfrey, one of the world's most powerful entertainers, always hosted her daily shows in the U.S. but on December 14, 2010, in a big co-branding venture with the Sydney Opera House, Oprah Winfrey and her team of 300 including guest John Travolta and loyal audience members, Tourism Australia, Qantas, Tourism New South Wales, Tourism Queensland, Tourism Victoria and Network 10 presented the *Oprah* show in the Sydney Opera House (*Wall Street Journal*, 2010). A number of very strong brands are involved in the venture—Oprah Winfrey, Sydney Opera House, Sydney, Australia (in this case for leisure travel rather than business travel in the first place), and this venture strengthens these brands in a clever way. First, it generates a lot of media attention at low cost. Since the combination of Winfrey and the Opera House in Sydney is new and interesting to media users, many channels will present this freely as news. Second, it positions a brand in relation to other brands that represent desired values. The Oprah Winfrey Sydney visit cost taxpayers at least AUD 3 million (Bryant, 2010; Carswell, Byrnes, & Fife-Yeomans, 2010; Fenner, Paton, & Saminather, 2010)—obviously a low price for the 'Oprah effect': It has been estimated that the worth of exposure for Australia is over AUD 83 million (Bulbeck, 2010).

An old-fashioned approach to how the public sector should spend money suggests that the money spent on the project was if not waste something that is not a public sector responsibility. The new, emerging market-based logic suggests that states, cities, counties and regions are responsible for, and will enjoy a lot of benefits through spending tax payers' money on marketing. Numerous individuals belonging to earlier generations—e.g., Oprah Winfrey and Dr. Phil—take advantage of this new market-based logic, but they did not grow up with it. For the Generation Y cohort, the market-based logic is something natural.

In any societal sector—schools, primary health care—competition has forced almost every organisation and institution to tell people why they exist and what they can offer in an increasingly cluttered media space. Actors identifying a basis of competitiveness that appeals to consumers have an advantage—a school that understands the power of localisation, a hospital located in an area with many qualified workers, or a city that understands that paying for promoting a celebrity that is visiting the city may be a very smart way of using taxpayers' money.

THE MARKET-BASED WAY-OF-THINKING SUGGESTS COMPANIES AND INDIVIDUALS TO DEVELOP COMPETITIVE ADVANTAGES

The market-based way-of-thinking suggests not only companies but also individuals to profile themselves and develop competitive advantages.

A more globalised economy, faster communication, new vehicles for dispersing knowledge and substantial demographic change makes it necessary for every organisation—they may be multinational companies, small and medium enterprises, public organisations or NGOs—and individual to focus on developing competitive advantages and profiling the offer, both in relation to the labour market and to the consumer market. For Generation Y individuals, one's own performance and career ambitions take place in a market context, and they know that they need to stay competitive in the labour market to maintain long-term attractiveness.

With the enormous amount of information and opportunities that are available, modern citizens need effective tools to make the right decisions—that's why attractive brands have become increasingly important and there are no signs that this will change in the future. The more global the world, the more opportunities there are and the faster the pace of change, and the more important for selling companies, employers, municipalities—and individuals—to have a strong and attractive brand. A strong brand has been described as "the glue that holds the organisation together". Needless to say, personal branding is different from corporate branding in many respects. Firstly, few people have personal brands that are recognised among a large group of people. Second, individuals do not work systematically and in a formalised manner with brand development. Third, an individual can change direction at any time depending on what makes sense. An individual might change ideological direction and conviction, might get a burn-out, change jobs or move to another country. Organisations, on the other hand, suffer from inertia so changes are slower. However, the mechanisms that create strong brands also apply to a large extent to individuals, and the emerging—and vast—literature on personal branding emphasises the importance for individuals with ambitious career plans to be aware of these mechanisms (cf. Goldsmith, Ulrich, & Rampersad, 2009; Purkiss & Royston-Lee, 2009; Spillane, 2000; Wilson & Blumenthal, 2008; Vickers et al., 2008). A Generation Y individual is likely to see branding as something natural and have less doubt when it comes to applying a market-oriented, branding perspective on one's own performance. Says one typical

Generation Yer: "We are used to promot[ing] ourselves, we learned that in school and our parents told us 'you must take the chance and show what you can, don't be that shy' . . ." (male, born 1984). University teachers describe an "enormous change" that came with Generation Y. "When I studied in the mid 1990s, people were shy and didn't like to make presentations. Group work was seen as a source of trouble and we enjoyed having low demands on our performance. One decade later, I myself [am] a teacher surrounded by ambitious Generation Yers. And, with few expectations, they like making presentations, they appear to be very comfortable with being on stage compared to my generation" (male, born 1974).

A TOUGH MARKET CLIMATE

The market environment has changed, with Globalisation and Internationalisation as major macro environmental forces. At a more concrete level, companies have to deal with a tough market climate, e.g., high information and price transparency, well-informed and knowledgeable consumers with tools—and attitudes—that support them in putting many demands on selling companies.

As an increasing percentage of jobs are white-collar, strategic, immaterial jobs with difficult trade-offs, complex decisions to make and lack of time and supervision, the labour market increasingly asks for flexible and well-educated individuals with the skills and attitudes necessary to make clever decisions. Those jobs can hardly be handled without great talent. Organisations now have to deal with many demands on effectiveness, shareholder expectations, environmental considerations, supplying a nice work environment, reaching good results in branding and quality rankings, just to mention a few. The competition is often heavy both within the industry and from substitute products that emerge at short notice. Without a doubt, the awareness about the coworker's role in shaping the organisation's competitiveness is higher than ever before.

This situation raises high demands on coworkers' social skills, emotional intelligence, customer orientation and businessmindedness, or at least having a market-oriented approach in the way decisions are made. How coworkers talk about their employer becomes very important, for a number of reasons:

- Younger individuals change jobs more often than before, and are to an extent being stressed by not being attractive in the labour market. Thus, they are more open to moving on and changing jobs, which makes them more attentive with regard to what is being said about employers they might consider working for.
- A movement towards grassroots information in individuals' search for knowledge about just about anything—the performance of a vacuum

cleaner, the reliability of a mobile phone network, the service quality of a Kindergarten or a hotel—or the qualities of a future workplace. Online tools for gathering information and discussing such matters are getting better and better.

- The blurred interface between leisure and work time (not for all professions and jobs, but for many), an increased transparency about what people are doing (social media makes a contribution to this development!) and the attitudes of Generation Y to ask at short notice rather than being afraid of putting demands upon the employer or seller has created a new situation for selling and employing.

Thus, coworkers are becoming increasingly important in presenting the workplace to key target groups, and the company as provider of goods and services. From an image and market communication perspective, consumer and labour markets are overlapping, and coworkers are crucial in building reputation in both (cf. Parment & Dyhre, 2009).

The last bullet point above is crucial in understanding how consumer and labour markets function in the Generation Y society. Jobs are being mediated at after-work sessions, coworkers are being recruited at parties, and products are being marketed at events, early bird receptions and other social happenings. This is certainly nothing new—cf. a baby boomer car salesman who says he is selling most of his cars on the golf course—but the way it happens is new. Societal institutions and company advertising have lost some of their power while grassroots information has gained solid ground as a key information channel.

THE CHANGING FACETS OF MARKETING COMMUNICATION

Societal changes and changes in the market environment have contributed significantly to changing the facets of marketing communication. Many companies appear to lack an understanding of what is going on. With the emergence of Generation Y as skilled coworkers and powerful consumers, it is likely to be even more important for companies in years to come to reevaluate their marketing communication strategies.

Several major factors are changing the facets of today's marketing communications. Changes in communications technology are causing remarkable changes in the ways in which companies and customers communicate with each other, and has given companies new media for interacting with targeted consumers. At the same time, consumers now have more control over the nature and timing of messages they choose to send and receive. Consumers are better informed and more communication empowered, which is an important driving force in the development towards a more intensive use of grassroots information. Customers can easily connect with other consumers to exchange information and they also become increasingly good at evaluating the grassroots information. Websites based on grassroots information have become better at organising the information, thus making it more valuable to the user. For instance, the travel site www.tripadvisor.co.uk distinguishes between different travel groups—a great development, since leisure, family, business and romance travel have different evaluation criteria. This development is likely to continue. For instance, it would be good for the user to know the background and generic demands on criteria such as value-for-money, location and the level of standard in choosing a hotel. A person who hardly went on vacation before may be more than satisfied with a hotel that disappoints a frequent business traveller used to the service and location advantages of four and five star hotels.

Getting consumer attention and making them spend money is difficult, which mirrors manufacturing overcapacities in many industries (cf. Parment, 2008a). While mass marketing techniques might have worked before, there is now a need for market communication that stands out. Today's marketers can amass detailed customer information, keep closer track of customer needs and tailor their offerings to narrowly target groups.

Picture 4.1 Urbanisation and an overload of market communication messages make environments with thousands of messages increasingly common, particularly in big cities like New York (picture), Tokyo and Shanghai.

The public space has become overloaded with market communication messages. Schools, theatres and hospitals, earlier seldom arenas for market communication, are now subject to market communication and city centers particularly see an increasing intensity of market communication messages. It is increasingly difficult to get through the noise so everybody is trying to shout louder, find new methods or do something different to stand out. Employers have similar experiences with job applicants: They work more on their CVs and personal letters, expect faster answers and do not hesitate

Picture 4.2   Market communication takes new ways to make a difference and stand out in a public space overloaded with messages.

to call the recruiter several times to promote themselves and raise questions about what the employer can offer (cf. Barrow & Mosley, 2005; Parment & Dyhre, 2009).

In some respects, however, labour markets are different. Like consumer markets, where power has shifted from companies to consumers, employees are strong now and have a great deal of power in relation to employers. This applies particularly to qualified Generation Y coworkers, who see themselves as important for the employer, not only the other way round. However, in labour markets, loyalty is an inherent characteristic and the flexible and market-based attitude of Generation Y does not mean they will change jobs continuously. A relation to an employer is something different from the often misused conception of customer relationships. It has a memory and backlog. A consumer can be rude in relation to a company, and it will most likely be forgotten or at least not made public—most companies with thousands or millions of customers have several cases of rude customers every day. An employer–employee relationship is more difficult to cease, and even if an individual changes employer, she or he will have the former employer in the CV for the foreseeable future. In addition to the fact that the relationship is much more intensive during the employment period, the relation is likely to continue in any form after the employment is finished. The former employee may buy products from, do consultancy projects with, be in an expert panel for, talk to the press or friends about, or in some other way continue the relationship, might it be initiated by either the employer or the employee.

THE SHIFTING MARKETING COMMUNICATIONS LANDSCAPE

Just as mass marketing once gave rise to a new generation of mass media communications—outdoor and newspaper advertising, television commercials, event sponsorship, etc.—the emergence of new technology has in the last decade or so given birth to a new marketing marketing communication landscape. Although television, magazines and other mass media remain very important, their dominance is declining. In the best case, new technologies makes it possible for marketers to reach, and have a conversation with, consumers who are consuming not what is force-fed to them, but exactly what they want."[4] Shows can be seen at their regular times or when you want (with or without the commercials), on the XPeria or iPhone. Some 'TV' programs aren't even on cable or network or satellite: They are being created just for Internet viewing."[5]

As mass media costs rise, advertising clutter increases, and viewers use video on demand and systems to skip past disruptive television commercials, some skeptics even predict the demise of the old mass media mainstays—30-second television commercials and glossy magazine advertisements. There is a substantial risk of companies spend their marketing money in a way that give limited effect—the number of television channels increases over time and so does the number of magazines as well as the number of magazine categories. Covering the market through these traditional means appears increasingly difficult and expensive. And the target groups—the desired customers—may not pay attention to the companies' attempts to communicate with them. Bob Garfield is one of the proponents of a scenario of a future fundamentally different from now, and he suggests: "a post-apocalyptic media world substantially devoid of brand advertising as we have long known it. It's a world in which consumer engagement occurs without consumer interruption, in which listening trumps dictating, in which the internet is a dollar store for movies and series, in which ad agencies are marginalised and Cannes[6] is deserted in the third week of June. It's a world, to be specific, in which marketing—and even branding—are conducted without much reliance on the 30-second spot or glossy spread. Because nobody is much interested in seeing them and because soon they will be largely unnecessary" (Garfield, 2007, p. 1). This would be a very negative future for the traditional marketing and advertising industry. And many large advertisers are shifting their advertising budgets away from network television in favor of more targeted, cost-effective, interactive and engaging media.

In the future, a likely development is a polarisation of marketing and advertising into practice that really adds value, and practice and campaign that do not. The former will most likely have good chances to be viable in the future by seeing beyond current practice, understand what is going on in the popular culture and in consumers' minds, and by coming up with ideas and campaigns that stand out and draw consumers' attention to the desired brands and products. The latter, less qualified marketing practices, will not be much ahead of the bread-and-butter knowledge available among advertising buyers and on the web, thus agencies, consultants and others engaged in this category are not likely to stay viable.

There is a certain element of inertia in companies' practices, and this applies also to marketing and advertising spending. Broadcast television and other mass media still capture a large share of the promotion budgets of most companies' marketing budgets, a fact that is not likely to change quickly. Although some, e.g., Garfield (2007) quoted previously, may question the future of the 30-second television spot, it's still very much in use today. Thus, it seems likely that the new marketing communications model will consist of a shifting mix of both traditional mass media and a wide array of new, more targeted, and more personalised media. The challenge for traditional marketers is to bridge the "media divide" that often separates traditional creative and media approaches from the new ones. For instance, the much discussed "social media", is it really something new? People have always been social so what is new with social media? And marketers have used the social dimension of marketing, not as much as now but it has been used.

It is not easy for a marketer to choose between running an event targeting Generation X families, a newspaper advertisement, and starting a Facebook group. This is obviously a challenge for many marketing managers, consultants and PR and advertising agencies—balancing the traditional with the new or, put differently, balancing the old, stable and safe way with Internet advertising and other emerging channels. Contrary to what many people may think, the effects of the latter are relatively easily measurable. However, from an overall perspective—measuring marketing effectiveness—the effects of both old and emerging media are difficult to measure.

Before a marketer eliminates the traditional, costly marketing channels, it is crucial to understand which industry one operates in and how consumers use media. Also the emerging channels may be overexposed with marketing messages and although it is often easier in new channels to target exactly the desired customers, the broader approach of traditional media also generates advantages. Some traditional marketing insights remain, e.g., that strong brands are built through broad communication—also those who can not afford or for other reasons are not likely to buy the brand should know what it stands for and thus contribute to building it—and that attention is crucial in communicating a message.

TRADITIONAL MEDIA MAY STILL BE USEFUL

Some newspapers report an increasing number of young readers, and one explanation may be that they are getting tired of the overexposition of marketing messages on the web (cf. Kotler et al., 2011). Sites like YouTube and Facebook started with little advertising but have over time been cluttered, just like many other channels. "A local politician added me, I thought we were friends, but obviously, all his Facebook communication is about winning the next election. Tiring!", says one Facebook user. Recommendations and links may be sponsored and users do not really know whether the recommendations are commercials, friends ("friends") who earn money by recommending products, or genuine help from friends. Newspaper websites increasingly present front page content that appears as editorial material at first sight, but prove to be advertising for those who take a closer look. Moreover, to maximise the number of clicks and advertising income, users are often asked to click more than would be necessary ("The winner of the EM competition—click here to see who it is").

A tricky balance in advertising is that on the one hand, it should be nice and in line with the corporate identity and brand profile, however, messages that are too nice and irritate nobody may result in limited advertising effectiveness. Many magazine ads are very unprovoking, which may limit their effect. By having a provoking headline or punch line, and a nice message, advertisers can get a lot of attention at a reasonable cost.

Box 4.1   The Daily Newspaper—Something for Generation Y Readers?

So there are obviously advantages with traditional media, and they may be very important in communicating with Generation Y. To take the newspaper as an example, it is easy to argue that it is an excellent market communication tool—provided the advertising has an appeal. First, the reader is relatively focused on the newspaper and did make the choice to read it. As a contrast, outdoor advertising may not be noticed (the consumer just walks or drives by) and television commercials irritate many consumers. With a digital box a consumer can choose not to watch the commercial, while nobody really expects a newspaper to have no advertising. Consumers like and want non-commercial information and knowledge. Good traditional newspapers have a solid journalistic foundation, with high integrity, and are not likely to compromise with the ambition to provide high-quality journalistic articles. Despite the criticism against traditional newspapers which often work under scarce resources compared to a few decades ago, many journalists working for major newspapers have critical thinking and a drive for revealing truths in their mindsets.

"If I call the editorial office and say 'hey, Mercedes wants to buy four full pages if we write something about their new S Class car' they will never accept that. The editorial office decides what they will write, and often with a short planning horizon. You never know what will happen around the world, thus you can't guarantee that a planned editorial content generates a particular level of attention. The editorial office may change their minds and say 'this stuff will not be published until tomorrow'. If they plan to write about something, we'll know, and if it is an enclosure, we are 100% sure it will be published, but they don't tell us what they will write. So we can't call Mercedes and say 'We'll praise your new car. Please buy four full pages from us,'" says Jesper Olsson, Manager of Dagens Nyheter Commercials, the leading Swedish newspaper. Dagens Nyheter's statistics suggest that the majority of the 35,000 new subscribers in 2009 were born in the 1970s and 1980s.

Moreover, newspapers have become customer-oriented, a reflection of a more competitive market for advertising and more demanding advertising buyers. In the old days, the newspaper industry was very order- and sales-driven as the unthreatened channel to use for many types of information and marketing messages. However, today there are so many channels and choices on *where* the ad is to be published, offline or online. "Now, the customer has many choices and demanding customers even make us create new solutions", says Matthias Sånemyr, Sales Manager at Dagens Nyheter Commercials.

An increasing number of companies understand that recruiting the right personnel is crucial to company success, particularly among Generation Y individuals. The increased focus on appealing emotionally to those people looking for a job—something that is particularly pronounced among young people—means that job ads are becoming increasingly thought-through to create the right appeal among the desired audience. And job ads are read also by people not looking for a new job, just like many real estate ad surfers don't

Box 4.1 (continued)

necessarily plan to buy a new apartment or house. Or the person reading the ad may look for a job in a fundamentally different industry. Nonetheless, they see and read the ad, if it stands out. "Our customers are sometimes getting surprised. For instance, Hymer Center Örebro, Swedish importer for Hymer and Carado motor homes and caravans, was looking for new employees and put an ad in a few newspapers. As a result, they got many customers visiting their showroom saying 'we saw your ad, and we are happy to see that your are doing so well.'" Looking for new employees sends a clear signal to people reading the newspaper: This company is doing great, and needs more people. It may create new sales and also tell existing customers that they made a good choice buying from a viable company.

COMMUNICATING WITH GENERATION Y

To have a strong relation with Generation Y consumers, it is appropriate to start communicating with consumers at an early stage, and this is for several reasons.

The younger individuals are, the more flexible they are likely to be in their brand preferences. With increasing age, individuals have more information about specific brands and attitudes develop during the life cycle, which normally makes it increasingly difficult to change consumers' attitudes with increasing consumer age (Söderlund & Parment, 2010).

Students are in many cases a target group that might be reached effectively and efficiently. At an early stage during the student years at a university, individuals are often not very well informed about brands related to the industries and contexts the study programme is preparing students for. Students certainly know a lot about consumer brands that are being extensively exposed in television and other venues of the popular culture. However, law students, business students and architectural students are likely to have a limited knowledge about future employers, so there is a high potential involved in communicating with them as early as possible during the study years. During the student years, people are often open-minded and develop their values and attitudes—which is actually the basic idea of going through a university educational programme. In this process, communicating with them and building relations and brand reputation is likely to be effective for a number of reasons. Firstly, it is a lot easier to change people's attitudes at this stage compared to later. Studies indicate that as people get older, they get more set in their ways and their brand attitudes acquire a stronger anchorage in their mindset. Second, it is comparatively cheap to communicate with young people since particularly if they are students, there are many ways of communicating with them effectively and efficiently, e.g., through campus activities, supporting student organisation and organising student events. Normally, student organisations, guest lectures and student events are cheaper to organise than similar activities for working professionals. Third, staying in close contact with students gives non-biased feedback from a key customer and employee group, which is invaluable for most organisations and should be given high priority by managers (cf. Zupko, 2007).

Student contacts have a very strong focus on social relations, which is further emphasised by the fact that students have fewer and less stable brand experiences. An organisation not belonging to the top ranked employers and product providers in its industry may benefit substantially from sending the right representatives to student events and lectures. Improvements in brand perception are likely to come faster than if the same amount of resources is spent on working professionals—however, the final decision depends on the desired age and profile of those people the organisation wants to recruit. Having a high representative-to-student ratio in student fairs has proven to be a great driver of success providing the right people are there (cf. Parment & Dyhre, 2009). The higher the number of representatives, the higher the likeliness of coming into contact with the right people, not only because the chance of coming into contact is higher, but also because more representatives means a greater variety of different personalities, ages, positions, etc., which makes it possible to catch the attention of a greater variety of potential employees.

To conclude, having a strategy and being selective is crucial to success. Without a strategy, the efforts to attract students may be expensive but have little result. If the wrong people are chosen, the employer brand will lose attractiveness. If the right people are chosen, they are likely to make a significant contribution to the employer brand by vitalising the organisation and its working procedures.

THE SHIFTING POWER BALANCE BETWEEN COMPANIES AND CONSUMERS

A key explanation to the changes in the market environment in its broadest sense, and to why the market logic has gained foothold in an increasing number of societal contexts, is the shifting power balance between companies and consumers. Regardless of age, consumers are now having more power in relation to companies than any time before in modern history. Most companies now offer customer call centers, customer treatment programmes, generous return policies, extended warranties and other services, created and run either to gain a competitive advantage, thus driving operating costs and customer expectations, or undertaken to avoid being competitively disadvantaged. It is not uncommon that companies are even more generous than they claim to be. Sometimes it takes extreme forms.

Radisson offers a 100% guest satisfaction programme. Some supermarkets, well aware of how expensive it is to recruit new customers, take all competitors' discount coupons.

A few decades ago, universities seldom undertook marketing activities beyond informing, e.g., through publishing catalogues with information on courses and educational programmes. This practice reflected the power balance at the time: There was a scarcity of university courses and difficult to get admitted. Individuals were happy to get admitted and universities were seen as authorities—like to a varying extent doctors, bank staff, car mechanics and Kindergarten managers. Today, everybody offering services is under constant customer surveillance—whether it is a doctor, a car mechanic or a high school teacher.

How did this new market-based logic come about? Gradually, power has moved from companies to individuals and this transition is driven by state deregulation, increased competition and individuals' attitudes. The latter are increasingly exploring new opportunities and less and less being loyal for its own sake.

YOU CAN'T DECIDE WHEN YOU COMMUNICATE!

A key insight in market communication, and also the very reason a solid communication strategy has to be founded in the organisational identity, is that a company, a public authority, a church, a school or any other type of organisation can not decide when to communicate and when not to. Consumers and coworkers are discussing their employer or preferred provider with friends, relatives, friends' friends, colleagues, customers, etc.—and this is hardly possible to control. Generation Y individuals increasingly see grassroots information and first-hand knowledge from employees and customers of a company as a key and reliable source of information, a development that is emphasised by the overload of messages in the public space.

It's becoming increasingly *difficult to communicate non-authentic messages*. Measures implemented to control the employer brand communication are only likely to work if the communicated message is authentic. Attitude studies may help in this respect: If employees (internal attitudes) and different target groups (external attitudes) like the organisation, that makes it possible to have some control over the attitudes as a starting point in communicating the employer brand. (Parment & Dyhre, 2009)

BRANDING: A BALANCING DILEMMA

As has now been made clear, branding is an inherent and defining aspect of today's society and market environment. A strong brand draws its advantage from *identification*, *consistency* and *attractiveness*. To achieve the advantages, one needs to know the organisation and its strengths and weaknesses, how to put it together to a consistent and attractive whole and then communicate it to the world around.

Some organisations have an inherent ability to attract employees, customers and other stakeholders. These organisations are good at bringing together and presenting the good sides of the organisation and what it stands for in a way that is seen as authentic and attractive by those who are the target of the message. Generation Y individuals particularly dislike marketing and other messages with little or no correspondence with what's really going on.

Strong brands always build on a consistent realisation of a few bearing ideas, which are implemented throughout the organisation. There is always a tension between the integrative top-down perspective, and ideas that are brought forward to make units and divisions closer to the market (cf. Castrogiovanni & Justis, 1998; Coughlan, Andersson, Stern, & El-Ansary, 2001; Parment, 2009a). This tricky balance is sometimes referred to as a dilemma of *balancing global integration and local responsiveness*, a framework assuming that international marketing decisions mean tricky trade-offs between adapting to local market conditions on the one hand, and reaching the efficiencies that standardisation across countries and regions imply (cf. Grein, Craig, & Takada, 2001; Haugland, 2010; Roth & Morrison, 1990; Parment, 2011; Spender & Grevesen, 1999).

Ideas such as 'we must listen to all our branches'; 'we need to adapt to what local offices are used to' or 'the London approach doesn't work here in little Darlingtown' are commonplace and should be dealt with. However, few successful companies have made local adaptation the overriding branding and control ideology. Giving too much consideration to local initiatives may take a lot of management time and make the organisation difficult to control, thus harming the opportunity to implement a strong brand (cf. Nilsson, Olve, & Parment, 2010). In the worst case, the organisation may end up in a situation which makes it very difficult to control:

> If all local initiatives are encouraged, then the company may become too sprawling; and decentralised, poorly-coordinated actions which lack relevance for the aims of the organisation bring dubious benefits. Holding the activities together, developing strategies, and basing the control system on these requires someone who is strong enough to generate enthusiasm and a feeling of urgency, of trust, and of faith in the future. Many people perform at their best when being led. (Nilsson et al., 2011, p. 123)

The process of building a brand that maintains its strength over time has a strong top-down emphasis. However, this does not mean that the communication is one-sided. The brand process benefits from feedback opportunities and safe avenues for expressing opinions and concerns among customers, employees and other stakeholders. However, all brand content and brand emphasis must be dealt with in relation to the overall company and brand strategy to make sure that the brand message sent is consistent across all communication channels and over time (cf. Birkigt, Stadler, & Funck, 1992; Parment, 2009a).

Decentralisation and a high degree of freedom for units and departments to create and apply their own principles and strategies in areas related to branding may be a problem also in the realms of employer branding.

> When I joined Novartis, recruitment advertising strategy was decentralised and as a result was inconsistent. Each department and region recruited locally, so there was little coherence with the overall brand. To have uniform advertising in recruitment is vital to the success of the employer brand.[7] (Veronica Foote, Global Head of Staffing, Novartis)

Web sites are a key source when individuals seek and apply for a job, and a fragmented brand experience is likely to make the target of the communication confused about what the organisation stands for. Making the brand appear similar across sites, units and countries may not only facilitate communication, but also save a lot of resources. Consider the case of 50 hotels, 75 car dealers or 90 supermarkets representing the same brand. If every unit creates their own website or advertising design, it certainly means a better local adaptation, but from the perspective of the overall brand and also from a cost perspective, a centralised strategy would be more effective. Nonetheless, particularly in very decentralised organisations with different client structures in different market areas, there must be room for some local initiative, but this can still be created in the framework of a centralised body.

CONSISTENCY AS THE FOUNDATION OF A SUCCESSFUL EMPLOYER BRAND

In the consumer's mind, messages from different media and promotional approaches all become part of a single message about the company. Conflicting messages from these different sources can result in confused company images, brand positions, and customer relationships. The emergence of grassroots-driven information is likely to result in increased problems with conflicting messages for many companies. All too often, mass media advertisements say one thing, while a website driven by user-generated data sends a different signal, and dealers' attitudes seem out of sync with everything else (cf. Parment, 2009a). Generation Y is sensitive to inconsistencies between what is being claimed and the everyday experience, and between messages in different channels. "If a company makes some corporate responsibility claims, and coworkers don't live up to them, it's a false claim and I would never consider working for such an employer", says a Generation Y individual.

Being consistent in communicating the brand can not be emphasised enough, and a great deal of branding literature emphasises the need for conceptual homogeneity (cf. Birkigt et al., 1992). Branding theorists emphasise that consumers and other stakeholders automatically integrate brand messages (Birkigt et al., 1992; Duncan & Moriarty, 1997). In a brand context, Kapferer (1997) like Achterholt (1988) emphasises the communicative role of all the organisation's activities: "It must be known by all" (Kapferer, 1997, p. 28); "Man kann nicht nicht-kommunizieren" (Achterholt, 1998, p. 39). Similarly, Kapferer views brand identity on the sender's side, and brand image on the receiver's side in a communication model. In this way, identity precedes image. Kapferer (1997) views corporate identity as the underlying meaning of the organisation: "Corporate identity is what helps an organisation, or a part of it, feel that it truly exists and that it is a coherent and unique being, with a history and a place of its own, different from others" (p. 91). The focus on brands and immaterial values which have grown stronger in the society might be translated into an advantage for organisations that communicate a clear identity.

Authors on brands stress the need of developing long-term strategies that involve all the company's areas of communication, which goes further than focusing on brand identity: The emphasis on the long-term is a criterion inherent in all attempts so strengthen or reorientate a brand. Kapferer (1997) argues that as all communication from a company is based on trustworthiness, a desired image must be well anchored in the company philosophy to establish a brand identity consistent over time. "Too often brands are examined through their component parts: the brand name, its logo, design or packaging, advertising or sponsorship, the level of image and brand awareness or, more recently, in terms of financial valuation. Real brand management, however, begins much earlier, with a strategy and a consistent, integrated vision. Its central concept is brand identity, not brand image. This identity must be defined and managed and is at the heart of brand management" (p. 18). Kapferer takes a view similar to that of Birkigt et al. (1992); the roots of a brand are found in a consistent long-term company strategy, which entails focus on philosophy and consistency rather than on the content of specific activities. Decisions will then be guided by the brand philosophy, thus securing consistency. If the company knows the soul of the brand or the corporate identity, and the brand is understood in a way that is consistent with the identity, it may give the company opportunities to try new concepts and expand into new segments: "Knowing brand identity paradoxically gives extra freedom of expression, since it emphasises the pre-eminence of substance over strictly formal features. Brand identity defines what must stay and what is free to change" (p. 93). Thus, a company that knows its brand's core values and for which there is shared customer awareness of the brand may enjoy the freedom of trying new approaches that may appeal to Generation Y.

THE BRAND AS COMPETITIVE ADVANTAGES

A key overall advantage of an attractive brand is its role in developing competitive advantages. A brand provides the customer representation of particular advantages: "The brand is a focal point for all the positive and negative impressions created by the buyer over time as he comes into contact with the brand's products, distribution channel, personnel and communications" (Kapferer, 1997, p. 25). Olins (1989) defines the subject of corporate identity in similar terms—products or services, environments where the products are sold, information and behaviour. Since a brand reflects customers' and other stakeholders' experiences and impressions, manufacturers have reason to put effort into building a brand that reflects the manufacturer's competitive advantages. The literature on brands shares the view that brands are long-term engagements: As put by Kapferer (1997), a brand is a long-term vision which should not be confused with company strategy. Rather, specifying brand purpose consists of defining the organisation's raison d'être. Arnold (1992) defines brand strategy as part of the overall strategy to create sustainable competitive advantages: "The objective of strategy is a sustainable competitive advantage, which may come from any part of the organisation's operations. The market is the judge of this advantage. Brand strategy is the process whereby the offer is positioned in the customer's mind to produce a perception of advantage" (Arnold, 1992, p. 96).

Brands as an outward reflection of the organisational identity goes further than the perceived brand image. Birkigt et al. (1992) emphasise that (lack of) organisational identity may constitute a major impediment in corporate and market communications. With this perspective, a clear-cut corporate identity will facilitate corporate and market communications substantially. Kapferer (1997) suggests that identity prevails over image; the notion of identity should be seen as the core concept of brand management: "before knowing how we are perceived, we must know who we are" (p. 71). Considering the high expectations on transparency and authenticity among Generation Y individuals, taking organisational identity as the starting-point in developing a strong brand and an appealing culture appears reasonable. Founding the organisation's attractiveness on a solid identity may provide advantages in terms of saving resources, reducing confusion and making it easier to create, maintain and develop a consistent brand philosophy.

TAKING ADVANTAGE OF A STRONG BRAND

One avenue of branding is connecting specific brands with a context, a person or a culture. The widespread practice of product placement shares characteristics and motives with using celebrities in marketing—it aims at building a brand indirectly by presenting a brand in a context that makes it stronger and more targeted towards the desired public.

The main advantage of using such methods—that marketing takes place in an indirect and rather discrete manner—has grown stronger over time, in light of an increasing information density and message overload in the public place. For instance, the use of product placement—like for other more or less aggressive methods like SMS offers and e-mail marketing messages—has increased over time. In the 1990s, when *Seinfeld* was one of the most popular television programmes, the use of product placement was very limited. However, already at the time, celebrities showed up on a regular basis. Two decades later, product placement is commonplace in a variety of television programmes.

For the viewer or receiver of the message, market communication channels that make use of real people that the desired target group are aware of, like and in a sense have a relation to are more effective than anonymous models. As put by John Casablancas: "I understood that if a model had a story—was a real person with a name—then the value of the model multiplied by 10" (*Vogue*, 2010). Models—whether they started in fashion modelling, as actors or as popstars (like Victoria Beckham)—have a strong influence over consumption patterns. Sales for Bugaboo, a Dutch manufacturer of design strollers, took off in 2004 when Gwyneth Paltrow was photographed pushing the "Apple cart" (Bugaboo's logo is an apple) down a street in New York. *The Heat* magazine's style editor, Ellie Crompton, said in an interview at the time: "We were going to do a whole page of celebrities pushing them" (Hopkinson, 2005). It proved very effective at the time to make a loved celebrity use the product: "When Paltrow picked the exclusive Bugaboo Frog to push around baby Apple, the pram world went mad. Parents fled towards shops to pick up one for themselves, phone lines jammed with inquiries and sales soared. Hence manufacturers' burning desire to press their products on stars." Crompton believes that photographs such as those of Gwyneth, Stella McCartney, Sara Cox and countless others wheeling their matching buggies through London's parks have really influenced the rest of us. "Everyone else thinks it must be the most safe, most advanced and most covetable pushchair on the market" (Asthana, 2004). Professor Frank Furedi, sociologist and parent-watcher, suggests that the popularity of the pram is part of a wider trend. "Parenting has become so intertwined with your identity that the way your child looks is seen as a direct extension of yourself. Having a particular buggy is a way of projecting your own desires and fantasies to the rest of the world" (Hopkinson, 2005). Product placement does not only sell the basic products but also, in the case of child strollers for instance, accessories (Asthana, 2004).

Who would have thought about designed expensive child strollers, and involving media in the marketing to make celebrities use them, a couple of decades ago? This is one among many examples of how real people can multiply sales for a product. Fashion companies have the same experience—after a fashionista has been photographed with a particular piece of clothing, sales may multiply.

COMPETITIVE ADVANTAGES MUST BE SUSTAINABLE

An important criterion in developing brands is sustainability. Competitive advantages must be sustainable to be valuable (cf. Nilsson et al., 2011), and one inherent quality in a brand is its sustainability. There are a number of explanations why it is likely that a strong brand position will be maintained for a long time, e.g., Aaker (1991) who proposes the development of a loyal customer base as essential to sustainability: Customers represent and may strengthen the brand. Southgate (1994) emphasises the importance of all people in the organisation actively communicating the brand values to the potential customers: "[A strong brand is] defensive in that [it] will deter competitors from trying to steal the brand-owner's market, and aggressive in that a strong brand will actively communicate with potential consumers on a multiplicity of levels, giving them all sorts of seductive reasons to buy" (p. 17). Kapferer (1997) discusses the power of consistency, referring to the balancing act of staying with the brand values and identity while adapting to changes in the marketplace. This balancing act may be easier for a strong brand as it will have more freedom to try out new approaches, etc., as long as the brand values are kept. Thus, a strong ideological platform entails more freedom of expression.

THE RATIONAL AND THE EMOTIONAL—
TWO DIFFERENT VENUES?

In marketing and consumer purchase analysis, it is common to use the concepts of "rational–emotional," or "functional–emotional" to categorise consumers and their shopping preferences and patterns[8]. A strong tendency when comparing generations is that baby boomers are reluctant to put forward emotional arguments, while Generation Y individuals in general terms see emotional preferences and purchase criteria as something natural.

Aesthetics, pride of ownership and a contribution to the self-image are examples of emotional aspects, and these apply both in consumer and labour markets. Moreover, the boundaries between rational and emotional aspects are not always clear and may be subject to personal interpretations. A person driving an all-wheel drive car may refer to a variety of rational (easier to drive under poor weather conditions, safer, saves time) as well as emotional (image advantage, and—again—safer) qualitites. Feeling secure and safe have both emotional and rational grounds,

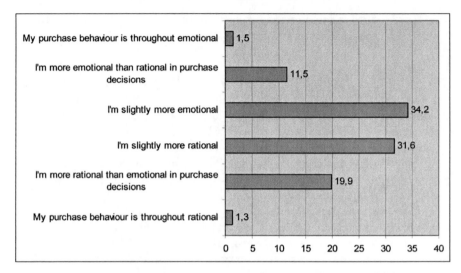

Figure 4.1   Generation Y on their purchase behaviour as rational/emotional. Percentage. Source: Generation Y survey.

and individuals are likely to have different ways of describing it depending on their values and preferences.

In many instances, there are a variety of arguments and criteria available, and a consumer may use the arguments that are appropriate in a particular situation. To mention a few examples: Somebody wanting a new and aesthetically attractive kitchen may refer to the high energy efficiency of new household appliances. A trip abroad may be suggested to buy cheap clothing, skiing and surfing equipment, consumer electronics equipment or wine. However, the savings may be smaller than the travel costs (and it's more difficult to return items if one regrets overshopping something). A person who finds the train more comfortable than travelling by car or air can use the argument of caring about the environment, which is likely to find appeal among most people.

In the labour market, a higher emotional appeal is likely to result in workers accepting lower wages, just like consumers pay higher prices for emotionally appealing products. Employers offering a strong consumer and employer brand, an international environment, and a good location are likely to have the opportunity to employ more qualified coworkers despite the fact that they (which, of course, is not always the case) pay lower wages (cf. Parment & Dyhre, 2009). In this respect, mechanisms in consumer and labour markets are similar. Consumers only buy products with a week brand if they get a price advantage, and employers with a brand that lacks attractiveness, reflecting a poor location, a non-appealing culture and poor leadership, will only have qualified employees if it pays a premium on the salary.

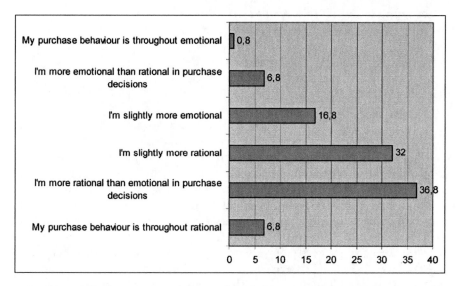

Figure 4.2 Baby boomers on their purchase behaviour as rational/emotional. Percentage. Source: Baby boomer survey.

All in all, the development over time is characterised by two findings:

- A stronger focus on individualism results in an increase in emotional and individualistic preferences in selecting preferred consumer brands and employers.
- A higher cultural and societal acceptance of emotional products and the higher price level they represent makes consumers increasingly used to emotional product aspects. As a consequence, the acceptance of and demand for emotionally appealing products and workplaces are likely to increase.

Figures 4.1 and 4.2, respectively, illustrate the growing strength of emotional purchase criteria among young consumers. Figure 4.1 represents Generation Y and, as a contrast, Figure 4.2 represents baby boomers, born in the 1940s and early 1950s.

OPEN AND EFFICIENT COMMUNICATION

Communication effectiveness is something every organisation that engages in marketing strives for. However, reaching a high level of effectiveness is not as easy as it might appear. First, traditional wisdom on the matter might not apply to the emerging society with Generation Y as an important target group. Second, with many of the emerging market communication channels, which are supposed to be effective, the outcome is difficult to measure, e.g., blogs, YouTube videos and pinpointing brand ambassadors in particular social settings. Using individuals, e.g., celebrities, is supposed to be effective but involves many considerations. First, we can not control their behaviour in general terms, and celebrities with a strong appeal among the desired customers sometimes do things that put not only their reputation, but also the reputation of the company that supports the celebrity, at risk. Second, it is difficult to measure the outcome of the cooperation since the engaged individual normally does a number of things that generate substantial media attention, but are totally unforeseeable when the agreement is written. Third, even individuals with a broad appeal have people who don't like them (even for reasons of envity!), so as opposed to many other marketing activities, engaging a celebrity may give some potential customers a reason not to buy.

Even though it is often difficult to know the outcome of marketing investments, discussing alternatives to existing strategies is likely to be fruitful. A powerful retail chain with operations across Northern Europe relies heavily on the catalogue, which has existed for almost a century. Relying on the catalogue in market communication appears to be a truth in this organisation, according to the marketing manager: "It is very difficult to get EUR 100,000 to develop the homepage. But we spend EUR 10 million on the catalogue every year. Imagine we wouldn't have the catalogue and I would step up to the CEO and say 'I have an excellent idea, what about printing 6 million catalogues at a cost of EUR 10 million, isn't that an excellent idea?'". Like most companies, this retail chain relies a lot on tradition instead of continuously re-evaluating the market communication approach. And obviously, many companies are doing well without a printed catalogue.

There is hardly anything more effective than employees who promote the organisation they work for, provided it happens in an authentic, balanced (not overselling) and nice manner. If people in the organisation are prepared to promote the organisation to their friends, families and social networks, the brand awareness and preference of the brand will benefit and the organisation is likely to strengthen its position among consumers, and also among potential coworkers.

At work, Generation Y individuals see open communication as something natural. They have grown up with open and fast communication and they are used to straightforward communication. As a contrast, corporate communication policies are often characterised by a certain element of slowness and formalism that makes open communication difficult. There is a lot of information that should not be shared openly, at least not without a foregoing discussion with responsible managers. However, in the case of information that should be shared openly, the system should operate as smoothly as possible with little formal procedure while it is being organised.

Box 4.2   Don'ts—Poor Information Management

An organisation with 3,500 employees shares information to employees by e-mailing middle managers who forward the message to the next manager and so on and so forth.

A typical message may be spread three or four times before it reaches the intended recipient. Even worse, there is no system in place to ensure that employees finally get the information. As there are only vague policies on e-mail communication in the organisation, middle managers may delay the information diffusion process by not forwarding the message until a few days or even more after they got it, they may just delete it as they don't like the message (there is no threat of punishment) or they may forget to read and forward it. The matrix structure of the organisation creates a situation where some people say they have two or even three bosses.

A unit facility manager says that "employees don't read e-mail messages from top management, they only listen to bosses they know, so we need to diffuse the information through middle managers". So employees may become important messages once, twice or not at all.

Particularly in big organisations, formal communication and extensive systems may be needed, but regardless of which system is in place, it is the attitude of the leaders, in terms of dealing with the information, that matters. Openness, transparency and trust lay the foundation of a good communication strategy, which is crucial when people use new and fast communication vehicles, easily find information elsewhere and expect the organisation's information system to work properly.

BUSINESS MODELS THAT HAVE APPEAL IN THE GENERATION Y SOCIETY

Any company and, to an increasing extent, also other organisations that might have been protected from competition in the past, have to develop competitive advantages. To do that, a business model needs to consider the characteristics of current and future customers. Globalisation and new communication vehicles make it increasingly difficult to maintain competitiveness unless an up-to-date understanding of how modern customers think exists among management and coworkers.

If loyalty was the rule with earlier generations, Generation Y will explore new opportunities whenever it is possible and makes sense. Dissatisfied customers always had, and made use of, the opportunity to change supplier and brand, but it was less common to do it for the simple reasons of exploring a new opportunity or "for fun".

The increasing willingness among consumers to change supplier has made it increasingly viable for emerging competitors in an industry to make use of the flexibility and curiousness on the customers side—"it's fun to try out something new" or "let's see what other companies offer". This development has resulted in a lot of creativity in many industries. It was not until the low-cost air carriers emerged that airlines had the courage not to serve food for free during the flight. Airports were located relatively close to city centers until RyanAir applied the provoking practice of referring to a city not even close to where the airport was located: Flying to Frankfurt (Hahn), 140 km from Frankfurt am Main, Barcelona-Girona, 100 km from Barcelona, or Stockholm-Skavsta, 110 km from Stockholm, entered a new practice into air travel marketing. Generation Y grew up with this and because of the multitude of practices out there, they are analytical and skeptical at the same time as they hardly hesitate to change provider. The old tradition suggested airlines to be prestigious enterprises countries were proud of, a reminiscence of the old gold days of air travel, and most airlines were running a multitude of aircrafts, ready to fly to destinations of different range. RyanAir applied an entirely different business model: By only flying one aircraft model—the Boeing 737, costs for training and inspection could be kept down. Any aircraft can fly on any distance and administrative systems do not need to consider different seatings in different aircrafts as is normally the case (cf. Parment, 2009c).

Fashion clothing is another example of an industry that has been subject to a fundamental transition. Budget brands selling cheap clothing have been available for several decades in outlets and shopping malls, while high-end premium brands were available in city centers, along with speciality stores selling medium priced volume brands and upscale premium brands. However, this all changed with the emergence of fashion retail chains like Hennes & Mauritz and Zara. First, these stores were, despite of the apparent inconsistency if interpreted with the traditional industry logic, offering fashion clothing in city center locations. These were certainly not as good as existing premium fashion brands in terms of quality and design, however, the design appealed to a young audience and low prices made it possible and convenient to buy new clothing more often (the ecological effects of which were not taken as seriously at the time as they would be today). Second, by offering budget fashion shopping in city centers, Hennes & Mauritz and Zara got access to fashion-aware customers who would hardly show up at clothing outlets. This is a key explanation to why Hennes & Mauritz and Zara have been extensively represented in fashion magazines like *Cosmopolitan*, *Elle* and *Vogue*. Third, they applied a new fast fashion concept based on a quick response principle (see Jeacle, 2007). Instead of offering a spring collection and an autumn collection, with few or no products introduced in between, new products were introduced and processed from product development to being available in store in a few weeks. Customers enjoyed new clothing being available every week, which provided great opportunities to increase showroom traffic. Now there was reason for many fashion-aware consumers to visit the stores every week or maybe even more often.

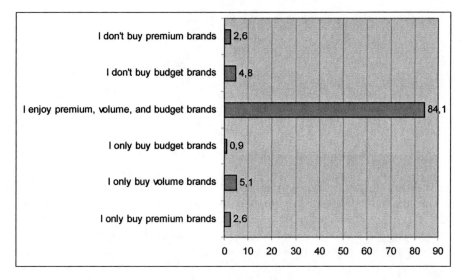

Figure 4.3 Most Generation Y individuals are flexible in terms of choosing budget, volume or premium brands depending on availability and the purchase situation at hand. Figures in percent. Source: Generation Y survey.

Business models should consider the transition of consumer purchase criteria—now, consumers mix premium, volume and budget brands—see Figure 4.3. A student may eat cheap pasta lunch and dinners most days— certainly nothing new—but enjoy the luxury of buying a pair of Seven for all Mankind jeans for £270. A young professional in her 30s, working as lawyer with a high annual income, may fly Business Class with KLM at work but enjoy RyanAir's cheap prices for purposes of leisure travelling. Some furniture might be bought from IKEA and other budget stores, while some other pieces of furniture are bought from upmarket retailers.

5 Generation Y and the Social Environment

Chapter 5 deals with the social environment, something that has always been a central venue for people in living their lives, but it appears to be particularly important for Generation Y. The interface between social environment and other central venues in life, e.g., the work environment, career planning and information processing, has become cluttered. The social environment now serves many functions, apart from its traditional meaning of providing pleasure and security.

As we will see, socialisation patterns have changed over time, something that is related to values and emphases in the society in which Generation Y grew up and came of age.

GENERATION Y—A SOCIAL GENERATION

Without any doubt, Generation Y individuals are, in general terms, social human beings—they enjoy socialising and they are forced to promote their social abilities for a number of reasons. First, few or no workplaces today accept coworkers with a high level of competence but a low level of social abilities. Regardless of whether an individual works with IT support, programming, HR policies or marketing campaigns, one needs to be a social and sufficiently nice human being. Not only at work, but also during leisure time, a coworker represents its employer. The times are gone when lack of a nice attitude could be compensated with a high level of competence. Second, the multitude of fora and channels for communicating means an individual should be prepared to deal with this. Whenever, wherever an employee is, there might be an opportunity to communicate, or even a necessity to do so. Third, individuals learn, at an early stage in life, that being social is an advantage. Working with others, using one's social network to get information for the solution of a problem, or working in projects are instances where social abilities count. Fourth, the social environment has become more multifaceted, dynamic and multinational. To be able to proactively navigate through this, one needs to have good social abilities. It has become increasingly common to meet people with a different background, different values and preferences and ideologies that differ from those one has grown up with. And organisations have increasingly come to appreciate the power of a multicultural attitude—something that makes the organisation better prepared for meeting different kinds of customers in different types of markets. In our globalised world, with local competitive advantages constantly being under pressure from international competition, social (and, of course, also in other respects great) employees will become increasingly important.

HOW ARE GENERATION Y INDIVIDUALS SOCIALISING?

A key aspect in understanding a generation is its way of socialising. Ever since the emergence of a youth culture around the 1950s, socialisation patterns among youths have been different from those of older people, and thus not really understood by older people. As was suggested in Chapter 1, Socrates suggested young people have "bad manners, contempt for authority; they show disrespect for their elders and love chatter in place of exercise; they no longer rise when elders enter the room; they contradict their parents, chatter before company; gobble up their food and tyrannise their teachers."[1] However, although this negative picture was created thousands of years ago, it appears clear that socialisation patterns were easier to understand and forecast before the emergence of youth cultures—and a new era started—that of teenagers hanging out, listening to music not understood by their parents, wearing clothing that appeared to set up parents, etc.

HOW THE INCREASING DIRECTNESS CAME ABOUT

Many people belonging to earlier generations—and not only baby boomers, but also Generation Xers—raise complaints about the directness of Generation Y. Instead of asking for permission, they do things. Instead of talking to peers and asking about company policies about something (office hours, official car, using Facebook at work or anything else) a Generation Y individual asks the manager directly. Instead of not telling the employer and current employees about a job one is applying for, Generation Y individuals tend to be open and straightforward not only with what they want but also with their plans. They tell their managers about their plans to move on to another job, take a second university degree or move to another city or country.

It is beyond any doubt that Generation Y individuals are more direct in their communication style compared to earlier generations. Driving forces in this development are a changed view on authorities, more choices and a stronger tendency to vote with the feet.

For any organisation, having coworkers who say what they expect, want and demand is an advantage. Less time will be spent on fear-based, non-constructive "thinking before acting" and there will be less frustration among coworkers since an open climate suggests anybody can ask any question at any time. In addition, managers and, in turn, top management, will get more feedback, of higher quality, from coworkers, which makes managers less frustrated and it will be thus easier to develop the job environment.

There are certainly problems with the transition to a state of openness and directness for many organisations, and to an extent it is linked to the changed view on integrity (see later in this chapter in the section on the changing character of social networks). Older coworkers may dislike the directness and see it as impertinent to address bosses informally or for young coworkers to have too much of a say during meetings. And their worries about young coworkers not taking integrity issues seriously may be right: As we will see, young individuals have a more open attitude towards sharing information—sometimes including information that is not feasible to share with individuals outside the organisation.

There are many driving forces in the development towards directness and openness, many of them treated elsewhere in this book (more choices, new communication channels, changed attitudes, etc.). One driving force that has changed the way individuals relate to and talk about applying for a new job is sites like LinkedIn. Even the most loyal coworker, at least as it seems, lists all job experiences and tells others that there are many other options. One's career track can easily be followed. And, maybe more importantly, members of LinkedIn suggest in public (anybody Googling them can see that) that they are looking for job opportunities and inquiries. That is different than before, when a coworker would normally not tell more than a few people about plans to move on.

SOCIALISATION PATTERNS AND THEIR IMPACT ON WORK LIFE

A central theme in understanding generations is socialisation patterns. Older colleagues of Generation Y individuals may react towards their manners and attitudes, but lack the understanding of how Generation Y individuals function in the workplace and how the differences between generations came about. This analysis of socialisation patterns builds on earlier chapters, i.e., the assumptions and descriptions of the society and market environment Generation Y grew up with.

Some key differences in socialisation patterns have a far-reaching impact on the way work is being done, and may also trigger generational conflicts. When older and younger coworkers share a workplace, there are most likely significant differences in how work is being done.

First, although Generation Y is comprised of social human beings in general terms, they may appear to socialise less with colleagues. For instance, they tend to be reluctant to have many meetings in the workplace or show up early and leave late only for reasons of being less senior. While older colleagues often apply an attitude of young colleagues showing they deserve freedom rather than taking opportunities to show up late or leave early, a Generation Y coworker may not even think about the problem of not coming first and leaving last. She has grown up in a society of plenty of opportunities and a different view on authorities compared to earlier generations, and this is manifested in the workplace. However, this should not be interpreted as young coworkers tending to be lazy. They just have another attitude towards rules and traditions. As for any generation, the opportunities of having flexible work hours vary with industry and organisation.

Working in an emergency room or supermarket gives little room for not showing up at work, however, even jobs that require coworkers being at work physically face changes that are accentuated with Generation Y entering the workplace. For instance, some hospitals have changed their staff planning from a top-down approach to a personnel-run system. Instead of a planning department making all the staff planning, which often resulted in complaints, doctors and nurses plan their own schedules, which provides some flexibility (there are legal constraints on working hours and length of work shifts) while still providing the workplace with the desired staffing. It proved that some employees wanted to work nights, during Christmas, in the summer or other periods which, according to the general discourse, "were hardly appreciated by anybody".

Second, the power of age and seniority has lost some of its influence of how work is being organised. The seniority principle suggests that individuals gather experiences and knowledge which accumulate over time, thus the older individual is always, by definition, more qualified. Many employer–union agreements rest on the seniority principle, thus providing a protection for older coworkers if the organisation is to cut down workforce. There are still many professions were seniority and years-in-office really count, e.g., lawyers, medical doctors and airline pilots. In these cases, few people would doubt that a decade or two in the profession makes the person more qualified, although the peak may come earlier than the point of retirement. For several other professions, e.g., salesmen, journalists, product developers, etc., young people living and acting in contexts of encouragement, customer proximity, qualified feedback, etc., may perform as well as, or even better than, older colleagues.

One example of the reorientation from seniority to qualifications in recruiting and promoting employees comes from the airline industry. Scandinavian Airlines Systems, to most people known as SAS, is a Scandinavian air carrier of significant size: It flies to about 90 destinations with a fleet of 134 aircraft (Scanorama, 2011). However, in the 1980s, SAS flew to more than 200 destinations so there has been a continuous and substantial downsizing of the SAS flight operations. The effect in terms of coworker structure is clear: They are getting fewer, and older. SAS has for several years considered other qualifications than seniority in deciding to promote individual coworkers. However, strong unions of SAS employees did not accept substantial deviations from the seniority principle. A case in which 15 air hostesses/stewards were undertaken from the principle of appointing based on the seniority principle was treated by the Swedish Labour Court in 1994. The court found that SAS did not violate the employer–union agreement by promoting younger, but more qualified, coworkers as air hostesses/stewards. The effect of the action was clear: SAS suspended the seniority principle, and market forces gained foothold in a company—and an industry—earlier controlled by unions to a high extent. With SAS's major profitability problems, an orientation away from the seniority policy towards decisions that are guided by SAS' needs for maintaining and improving competitiveness may also be in the employee's interest.

Third, the sources of information for carrying out work and making decisions are different from what they were before. The reason coworkers are increasingly asking friends, alumni network contacts, searching information and solutions on the Internet or just talking to somebody at the workplace without informing the boss is clear: The labour market has changed. Many industries have seen a sharper competition and need to have coworkers who work effectively and efficiently. The view on authorities and

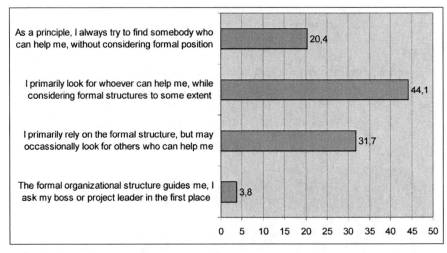

Figure 5.1 Generation Y individuals ask people they believe can help them in the first place, not the boss or people with the formal authority. Source: Employer Branding survey.

integrity has changed, and there are tools to communicate effectively with the desired individual/s.

As Generation Y individuals change jobs more often and plan to do so also in the future, they find stronger reasons to build their network independently from their current workplace.

Important to note, it is a myth that Generation Y in general is planning to change jobs very often and are unwilling to stay with the same employer for a number of years. Generation Y individuals who find the job appealing, and particularly if there are adequate opportunities to make a career within the organisation, are likely to stay. But their threshold for changing jobs is lower and organisations must work harder to make sure Generation Y individuals like the work environment. Although great employers will still get many qualified employees who stay with the employer for several years, from an aggregate perspective, Generation Y individuals will change jobs more often and have a smaller part of their social networks in the current workplace compared to earlier generations. And they will have great use of their social networks in getting inspiration, performing work assignments, sell products, create new projects and ventures and recruit new coworkers when they are in the position to do that.

All the changes described previously have been strongly influenced by socialisation patterns—in families, at school, during leisure time and as consumers. For Generation Y, the social environment is at the heart of just about any decision or activity in life and it is therefore crucial to understand this generational cohort.

Moreover, building on the idea of moving on, friends, family and colleagues alike may be crucial elements in the social environment that contribute to put pressure on an individual to develop, make a good career, change jobs, etc. It becomes increasingly evident to young people particularly that having a great social network is key to realising opportunities in life. A hobby musician knows that the social network is critical in getting songs uploaded on sites like MySpace promoted and somebody running a travel agency knows that having many contacts in the social network is a great marketing opportunity.

LESS ONE SIZE FITS ALL AND MORE MICROMANAGEMENT

A couple of decades ago, most people were living in *mass societies*: Life had a rhythm and individuals in general had a limited opportunity of influencing the rhythm and pace of life. Work started when the factory opened, or the work session started. Buses or other means of public transport transported the workers to the factory, and back when the work day was finished. Television programmes were available when they were aired—unless one had a video recorder, still an expensive luxury at the end of the 1970s. Grocery stores closed at regulated closing hours. Leisure activities were *offered* by the company, union, non-profit association or church providing it—at the time, users or parents of children attending the activities were hardly voting with their feet. There were few other opportunities and the acceptance for communicating dissatisfaction was limited.

All in all, in the past, one size fits all appears to have been the approach to many situations that influence people's everyday lives. Thanks to changes in the social environment and new technologies everyday life might now be used more efficiently—something that stresses some people but makes some others relax.

Box 5.1   Micromanaging the Day to Take Every Opportunity

If the bus is late, a sign will tell you and you will get 8 minutes to visit a pharmacy and buy pills, or a coffee at Starbucks. If watching *Midsomer Murders* at 4 p.m. on a tv channel doesn't fit your schedule, you can watch it on the channel's online Play channel 2 hours later. If there is a party or event and you hesitate to join, you can track participants in the Facebook invitation. SMS reminds you of car inspections, late flights, your dentist being on sick leave or a parcel that arrived at the local post office. Publishers apply print-on-demand and can offer any combination of book chapters from the publisher's books for a particular application. If there is a car accident, the GPS will tell you and you can call the office and tell you are late—in the past, the person didn't turn up and nobody knew why. There was no mobile phone for calling the office. RSS gives you the latest breaking news headlines from BBC, CNN, ABC or Deutsche Welle.

You can micromanage your life to maximise every opportunity.

It's increasingly up to the individual to handle this situation with an endless supply of opportunities and choices. Some people have a vacation message when they are out of office for 4 weeks during the summertime. Nonetheless, they answer e-mails in 10 minutes from their smart phone while sailing with their friends or family.

Also the changing character of many jobs increase the opportunities to multitask, have leisure time at work and have work at leisure time, or being in one location and having control of what is happening in another location. We can now micromanage our lives in a way that was impossible a few decades ago.

Where will this end up? Many older people are stressed by the changes, while it is something natural for the Generation Y cohort. One may ask what the changes really bring, however, reversing the development is difficult. A proactive person may find ways of benefiting from the changes—work more effectively, avoid traffic jams, watching the favourite tv programme after finishing work instead of interrupting work, showing up later at work, etc.

In some countries, and Scandinavia particularly, the state took more responsibility for people's lives before, and it's more and more left to market forces and individuals' own way to navigate through life.

The growth of micromanagement opportunities contributes to making individuals even more used to not waiting in queues, responding fast and late to invitations, checking information on the Internet, etc. Not only does the increasing number of choices in the marketplace change people's behaviour, it also gives rise to new opportunities and new opportunities to run even more microscheduled lives. As it seems, it appears unlikely that we will go back to the old society that existed before the changes described in this book came about.

THE CHANGING CHARACTER OF SOCIAL NETWORKS

A couple of decades ago, social networks for most people were local and required some formal position or status. A well known and recognised family, a formal education or membership in something like a church, a union, a political party or a trade association implied access to a social network.

The function of social networks is still the same—to provide contacts, solutions to problems, security and pleasure. Now and then, people have socialised and built social networks—as a strategy or with a more relaxed attitude—for these reasons and the mixture of reasons to socialise vary now, as they have always done. Some socialise to strengthen their social position, and sell more products from their furniture store. Others socialise for fun, or for reasons of spreading the gospel of a political, or any other, message.

However, in a number of respects, the facets of social networking have changed fundamentally. In the old society, social networks were offline, local and closed. Now and increasingly so in the future, social networks are online, international (or, at least, national), and open. This means individuals who are knowledgeable, and have a broad set of cultural and language skills, will more easily navigate and take advantage of the opportunities that social networks provide. The fundamental transition of social networks have a number of driving forces and effects and Generation Y grew up and came of age in a society that focused on the emerging characteristics of social networks.

First, *the Internet has fundamentally changed the preconditions for running social networks.* This applies both for networks run by organisations and peer-run networks. The former enjoy the easiness of communicating, the opportunities to control what is going on in online fora, etc., and the attractivity and directness that online interactivity results in. The latter particularly enjoy the increased opportunities to *create new networks through existing networks*—and the considerably lower costs of running the network/s. Not every Facebook group is a social network but there are definitely many social networks that would not have existed, at least not with the substance and communication intensity they have now, unless the Internet existed. University and company alumni networks—both have increased substantially in the last decade—professional organisations (e.g., GP doctors in the BeNeLux countries), Young Professionals networks and networks of political fractions (with connection to a major party or not) are instances were the existence of the Internet alone have fundamentally changed the preconditions for running the networks.

Second, socialising and using social networks to tell who I am to others is certainly nothing new, but the *opportunities of making socialising a personal branding venue is bigger than ever.* Facebook is one of the most obvious examples of how individuals can use the Internet to present themselves in the desired way, i.e., as a *personal branding channel.* Individuals tell people around—friends, "friends" (according to studies, many social network users are friends with people they do not know or have not even met) or anybody who is Googling versus searching him or her—what they like, what they don't like, political and religious convictions, favourite music, etc. Like in any marketing context, messages that are not connected to reality run the risk of not being taken seriously or even putting the person's brand at risk. And the existence of fake characters make people attentive and critical, something that is natural for Generation Y.

Third, the *changed criteria for getting access to those networks.* Family history, political party membership, living area, gender, age and other demographic variables often determined membership before. Now, networks are more open and not only are ideas more often grassroots driven but also criteria for getting access to the network. Like before, social aspects which are not very easy to conceptualise circumscribe social networking and criteria, which may be vague and attitudinal, for getting inside a group, context or club. Criteria and feedback are certainly getting more direct, but the fact remains that individuals may want to keep the exclusiveness of something, and thus may be mean towards individuals who attempt to get inside. More than ever, having the right attitudes and social skills to understand a particular social context are getting increasingly important.

Fourth, the *increasing number of social networks*, and the strong *tendency not to engage in something for a lifetime*, makes a significant contribution to the lack of loyalty in many social networks. Many NGOs, political parties, churches and other organisations—all of them certainly not being social networks in a strict sense, but the point is clear—used to have very loyal members. If one became head of the local trade organisation or chairperson of a church, the person was likely to stay at the position if not for a lifetime for many years. Many baby boomers and generations before them have kept such positions for two, three or even four decades. Not so with Generation Y. They have a different approach to prestige of positions and scaling down. To them, leaving a desired position is not seen as a loss of prestige, and just like they plan to change jobs more often than earlier generations, they are likely to take on and leave engagements for NGOs, etc., more often. This reflects their life philosophy of enjoying variations and new opportunities, while not wanting to stay in a position for too long a time. Today there are both top-down company and institution driven and grassroots organised social networks for just about anything, so there are many opportunities for Generation Y to realise their life and career plans through social networks.

Fifth, a *changed view on personal integrity*. In almost any industry or context, one can observe substantial differences among generations in the approach to what can be made public and not. At a major university, management introduced a tool that scans student assignments and thesis work for copying and pasting material from the Internet. Plagiarism is something older and younger faculty have similar attitudes towards, however, while younger collegaues (Generation X and a few from Generation Y) suggested "it's in everybody's interest, it's good for students who have nothing to hide", older collegaues (baby boomers) said "this is a severe damage to students' personal integrity. We must trust them and follow their work process sufficiently to make sure they are not copying anything from the Internet". Not surprisingly, students had no problem with having their documents scanned: "We have nothing to hide, it's good to know that nobody, including my writing partner, put something in the thesis that shouldn't be there". Many employers have problems with young coworkers publishing pictures from the work environment, company parties or even from parties with clients on the Internet. Needless to say, such behaviour might be a problem, particularly as many clients may still have the traditional view on personal integrity. As was discussed in Chapter 3, the interface between work and leisure time has become blurred, and these changes have contributed significantly to the changes in—and emerging problems with—social networks described here.

WHO CAN HELP ME SOLVE PROBLEMS?
THE SOCIAL NETWORK!

For the Generation Y cohort, social networks are crucial not only to make a good career and fill the leisure time with meaningful and enjoyable activities, but also to carry out every day work. An important driving force in Generation Y's new definition of how work should be carried out is the phenomenon of social networks. Individuals in social networks inspire Generation Y to move forward and change jobs, and social networks also give such opportunities, in addition to their role of helping individuals carrying out work. A person with a great social network is more likely to be able to solve problems that emerge and to find input and inspiration for dealing with tricky issues.

The upside of this development is that the new generation of coworkers question the way the organisation works and, moreover, ideas that are taken for given are put under investigation. This is likely to inject the organisation with energy and ideas that may improve its competitiveness as well as its attractiveness as employer. On the other hand, the risk of coworkers leaking confidential information or other pieces of information not suitable for transfer to a third party is higher than with earlier generations.

If my boss asks me how things are going, I always say 'yes, great', because she doesn't understand what I'm doing, and she'll probably sleep better if I say 'yes, great', she doesn't know my competence area and I always solve the problems that arise. (engineer at work, male, born 1980)

This quotation reflects *the transition from the boss as the person to ask, to a strong tendency for employees to use their social networks to complete tasks.* There are a number of driving forces that might be identified in this development—a changed view on authorities, the emergence of new communication tools, the growing importance of social networks, and a labour market that emphasises performance. At the end of the day, it is likely to be easier to solve problems and perform tasks if one uses the resources that social networks provide.

In recruiting personnel, it should be considered that by employing an individual, particularly if it is a Generation Y individual, the organisation also gets access to his/her social network. Not only from an efficiency point of view, but also from the perspective of recruiting further employees, and

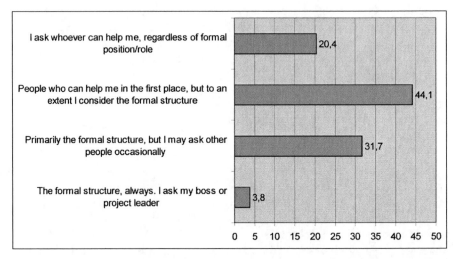

Figure 5.2 Question on whom Generation Y individuals ask in solving work-related problems and carrying out everyday work. As it appears, the social network might be more important than competence available among the organisation's coworkers. Figures in percent. Source: Employer Branding survey.

Box 5.2   The Employee's Social Network: A Great Marketing Opportunity

Employee's contacts in social networks may be an important asset for a selling company, and provide a number of marketing benefits. First, it makes the targeting better (provided the social networks available through coworkers have members of the desired target groups). Second, it is likely to be more effective and efficient. Third, it may create coworker motivation.

A company that is coming out with a new product may use coworkers' social networks to access the desired target group. Assume the company wants access to 100 young females interested in fashion for a product launch. The traditional way of doing it is to contact a media agency that is sending invitations to a few hundred young females who, based on some segmentation criteria, get an invitation. However, in bigger cities particularly, the high intensity of marketing messages, event invitations, etc., makes it difficult to reach a high positive response rate. In the organisation, there are likely to be a few young coworkers who have—close and more peripheral—friends interested in fashion. And these friends may in turn have other fashion-interested friends. Through personal invitations the percentage of invitation acceptance is likely to be high. The company will have no costs for buying contact details and the coworker will be motivated by having the opportunity to invite friends for an activity that means offering the latest products, free dining and drinking, opportunities for further social networking, etc. The company's consumer brand is likely to benefit from a target group-customised and positive event, and the employer brand is promoted through employees' realising themselves when inviting friends to an event.

Any company selling products to consumers may use their employees to market products. It is a central characteristic of *brand ambassadorship*: Employees are ambassadors of the consumer brand as well as of the employer brand. Employees socialise, discuss and represent the employer and the consumer brand through presenting products, providing solutions and by being a person who is liking and living the brand.

Having employees with social networks that fit the company's profile and strategy is likely to be a great advantage. And the fit should not be a problem for companies with a strong profile and high strategic awareness among managers and employees: They automatically attract individuals who fit with the company and its strategy (cf. Nilsson, Olve, & Parment, 2011; Parment & Dyhre, 2009).

having brand ambassadors promoting the organisation's products during their leisure time, it is likely to be an advantage. On the other hand, it becomes increasingly important to make sure that individuals who work for the organisation can manage the tricky balance between using their social networks on the one hand, and not transmitting information not suitable for third parties in such discussions.

THE SOCIAL NETWORK: A MULTIFACETED INFORMATION SOURCE

The fact that Generation Y individuals will change jobs more often than earlier generations, something that is supported by labour market data from many countries, at the same time as social networks become more important, will fundamentally change the balance between the employer's organisation and information from outside the organisation in a number of respects.

First, *individuals' loyalty may in many cases be higher to their social networks and alumni associations than to their employer*—assuming loyalty is defined as one-firm commitment or staying together for a long time (see the next paragraph and Figure 5.2). Relations in social networks are likely to last longer than the relationship to the employer, which will rather be part of the person's alumni experiences. The nature of social networks vary, as does their longevity. A university alumni network may last for a lifetime, as may family or church membership. A Young Professionals network is nothing for people after their 45th birthday, and political and union engagements may change during a lifetime as do many other social network contexts.

Second, *information searches for a variety of matters are likely to increasingly take place outside the realms of the organisation*. As suggested by Figure 5.2, Generation Y coworkers do not hesitate to investigate sources outside the organisation in solving everyday work assignments or solving problems. The more often an individual changes jobs, and the more the individual engages in different types of social networks, the more likely she will find the ideas, inspiration, information and knowledge needed outside the organisation. That, in turn, may reduce the individual coworker's commitment to the employer.

Third, both for reasons of a broader set of arenas for social networking, and individuals changing jobs more often, *an individual's friends are likely to increasingly be available outside the workplace*. If in the past one had many friends in the workplace, that is undergoing a change. The Internationalisation of the labour market has contributed to this change—while in the past, many people stayed in the same professional and geographical area for decades, now an increasing percentage of coworkers work in international organisations with offices or at least customers and suppliers in other countries. It has been proven in several studies that the number of social contacts a person is having during a year has increased significantly, and not only has the number of contacts increased but also the variety of people one meets. In the past, many coworkers had a large or even major part of their friends in the workplace—no surprise, since they worked for a long time in the same workplace and intended to stay for long. Not only the company one worked for but also the industry and job position hardly changed—most people stayed within their area of expertise. Today, people change jobs and move across traditional definitions of professions and job content in an emerging multitude of traditional jobs, mixtures of traditional and emerging jobs, and job positions that did not even exist a few decades ago. The high friend density at work was another reason to stay with the employer. In employee surveys, there are not seldom patterns indicating that employees are not really in tune with the organisation's strategy, etc., but like their department, which happen to be populated with people who have been working there for a very long time and may have problems getting a new job. Today, many Generation Y individuals and Young Professionals may have many friends at work, but they do not stay with the organisation for the reason of staying in contact with the friends. And there are many ways of staying in contact with friends once one has left.

Fourth, *new job offers will come from just about any source* inside or outside the organisation—career networks like LinkedIn, social networks like Facebook, career sites of employers one has applied for or contacted in the past for job matters, colleagues, Young Professionals networks, etc., in addition to traditional offline or online job ads. The current employer thus loses control over what the employee is being offered and may have difficulties getting through the jungle of job and career messages. In addition, some employers—inspired by the battle in the labour market for talented employees—direct so much energy to attracting external people that they lose the contact with existing employees (cf. Parment & Dyhre, 2009). That is a serious mistake: While the best of the current employees are staying in close contact with the labour market and all that it offers, in the worst case, the HR department does not notice how high the talented individuals' awareness of this is. Thus, the HR department runs the risk of becoming very reactive in trying to keep the talented employees once they are about to sign for another employer.

THE CHANGING FACETS OF LOYALTY

Loyalty is a complex concept and has in labour market contexts often been defined as a structural, easily measurable component that sets a number on how long a coworker stays with the organisation on average, i.e., the personnel turnover. However, loyalty also has an attitudinal meaning and may be defined as a feeling or an attitude of devoted attachment, catched by the widely used concept one-firm-commitment.

Loyalty in a consumer marketing context has been widely discussed and applied, e.g., by Dick & Basu (1984), Oliver (1999) and Reinartz and Kumar (2002). Also in the context of consumer marketing, the distinction between structural and attitudinal meanings of loyalty are made clear.

For Generation Y individuals, the social network fulfills many functions, i.e., being a core channel in finding a new job. As is suggested in Figure 5.4, the social network is important in finding a new job. Companies

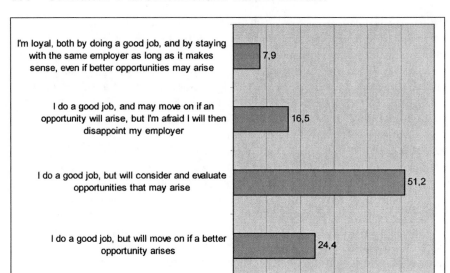

Figure 5.3   Loyalty—a complex concept. This figure represents Generation Y individuals' view on loyalty. Figures in percent. Source: Employer Branding survey.

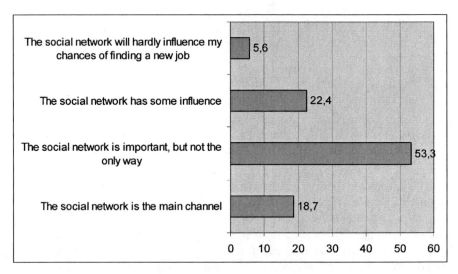

Figure 5.4   The importance of the social network in finding a new job. Figures in percent. Source: Employer Branding survey.

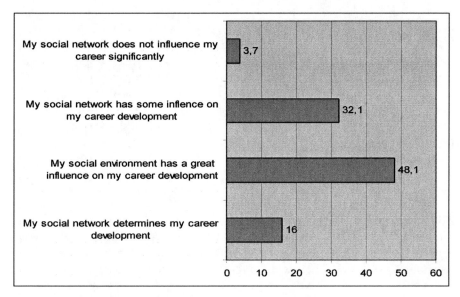

Figure 5.5   The influence of my social network on my career development. Figures in percent. Source: Employer Branding survey.

looking for applicants should be aware of the increasing power of grass-roots initiatives.

Also from an overall career development perspective, the social network has an important role. Some parts of the social network may follow the individual through her career, e.g., university alumni networks, and trainee alumni networks. There are smart ways for organisations to keep some control over networks. Knowing they will exist any way, the question is who is going to initiate and run the social network. Some proactive organisations, e.g., the Royal Institute of Technology in Stockholm, let students keep their e-mail addresses when they leave. There are several benefits with this approach. First, the organisation keeps the contact with all former students, providing they still use the e-mail address—but as they have their study colleagues there, they are likely to continue using it. Second, former students see it as a benefit to have a back-up from their alumni university through a channel that offers opportunities to stay in contact with alumni friends, receive job offers, event and course invitations, etc. Third, it is cheaper than seeking out, contacting and attracting the students later when there might be a higher need to do so than directly after students get their degrees and leave. An e-mail account does not cost a lot per user and year, while it has proven to be costly to build an alumni network once the contact with former students is more or less lost.

The *transition from the organisation's authority structure to the social network as the hub of information gathering* has some important implications. On the one hand, the competence of the organisation expands without additional cost. On the other hand, the organisation runs a higher risk that confidential customer information and business securities get disclosed and come in the hands of a wider circle of people who should not get access to it. Thus, while recruiting new coworkers, organisations should be aware of this integrity-related issue and try to capture the integrity attitudes of potential coworkers.

THE EMERGENCE OF SOCIAL MEDIA

The power and potential of social media communities for marketing mediums have been widely discussed in recent years. Social media platforms provide a great opportunity for information sharing, communication and relationship building and maintenance. Social media marketing is an interactive type of online advertising that uses the cultural context and user profiles of social communities, e.g., Facebook. There are also social media communities, e.g., forums—now there are forums for just about anything—and social news sites—websites where users submit and vote on news stories or other links, e.g., Digg.

As social networking becomes increasingly popular, both for social and professional purposes, it is important to distinguish between the two inherently different goals of networking. Even though the two spheres of work and leisure time converge for Generation Y individuals, they are still separate. And the very reason networking sites came about is often linked to one of the two purposes. Facebook, launched in 2004 at a time when MySpace dominated the social media market, began as a social networking tool for college students. LinkedIn began as a business network and disallowed opportunities to post photo albums or converse freely with the contacts. LinkedIn has expanded with social and business applications, thus allowing for functions known from Facebook, however, it maintains its identity as a professional networking community.

Still, Facebook is a highly social network, and many individuals use Facebook for social, private purposes and LinkedIn for professional purposes.

What does the rapid growth of social networking communities mean for marketing and branding? Obviously, companies should be aware of this development and what it means to them. First, the saturation of messages overall has increased, which may increase individuals' multi-tasking abilities but also put a certain amount of stress upon individuals. Social networking communities may be a stimulating and effective way of finding pleasure and organising a good life, but also a problem: Some individuals may find it difficult not to follow the always ongoing dialogue and the plenty of upgrades of what "friends" are doing. Second, the level of integrity decreases as individuals have become more open with what they do—in leisure time and at work—to others. Internet overall has fundamentally changed the opportunities of easily checking another individual or organisation: Where does she live? Where has she worked? What is her annual income? Who are her friends? What is her date of birth? Social networking communities contribute to making new generations used to a higher level of openness in the social environment. Third, it becomes a lot easier to encourage engagement in a particular interest, and finding friends that share the interest. There are groups dealing with just about anything—music taste, civil disobedience, political and ideological engagements, liking or disliking a hotel chain or local grocery store, celebrity fan clubs, etc. Fourth, career advancement purposes, initiated by individuals or companies, is a strong effect of social networking, which reflects the emerging power balance of qualified individuals having a strong power position in relation to potential employers. Fifth, it is an important marketing communication channel, with grassroots driven, quasi grassroots driven and company driven channels as opportunities—or threats—for the company.

Strong companies, brands and products are likely to benefit from *grassroots initiatives*, which translate into great advantages since users see grassroots information as polite and adequate sources, provided it has been organised in a good way. Also *company driven channels* are easier to establish with a strong brand or product: Network groups, etc., are likely to get numerous members, and many businesses now have fan pages on websites like Facebook, and give discounts and coupons that users otherwise would not receive. There are also *quasi grassroots initiatives*—communication that appears to be grassroots initiated at first sight, but there is a company behind that offers the communicator some benefits. Examples are "users" trying out new products, which they find "excellent", something they tell their friends, but without saying that they got money, free samples or other benefits from the company manufacturing or selling the product. It is certainly a matter of degree—ranging from free product samples to massive hidden campaigns, but companies run the risk of getting a poor reputation if social networking is used too heavily for product marketing purposes. On the other hand, doing it in the right way may be an effective way of marketing the company.

Being proactive is crucial to success. For instance, a proactive company that establishes its own company-run social network may enjoy the advantages of control and feedback for many years, while a reactive company discovers that current or earlier consumers or employees have established a network. It is then too late to gain control over the network.

There are several channels that are normally defined as social media. *Facebook* with its more than 600 million users (Ahmad, 2011) is the most powerful one, however, this may change in the future although Facebook's enormous database of users is a strength that is difficult to neglect. In Summer 2010, Facebook introduced a professional network function called

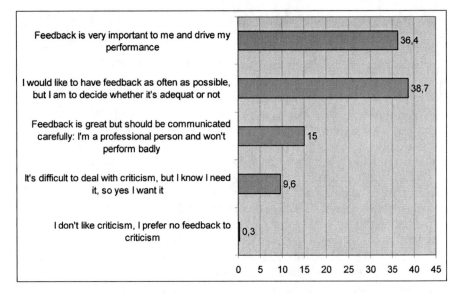

Figure 5.6 The majority of Generation Y individuals appreciate feedback—not only because they like it, but also because they feel they need to know how well they perform. Figures in percent. Source: Generation Y survey.

BranchOut, thus making use of its strength as a social networking community and using it for the purpose of professional networking.

All in all, social networking makes market forces stronger and is to the benefit of strong companies, but may be a serious problem for companies with lack of consumer confidence, dissatisfied coworkers, a weak brand or any other serious problem. Both positive and negative aspects of the company and its offers will be communicated faster, and more effectively through the broad reach of social networking channels. Social networking encourages interaction between consumers and companies, and also among consumers, and it may strengthen a brand's profile or undermine it depending on what is discussed, how and by whom. It will become more obvious with social networking what the company really stands for and how the products are actually being considered by consumers.

Social networks give many branding and marketing communication opportunities. Leading companies are leveraging social media participation for a number of reasons, cf. Figure 5.7, brand building, customer recruitment and new product introduction being the most important reasons.

As suggested by the survey presented in Figure 5.7, the percentage of leading companies using social media platforms is high: Fortune 500 represents a mixture of companies operating in a multitude of industries. As it seems, also conservative energy, financial and healthcare industries are attempting to enjoy the advantages of social media marketing.

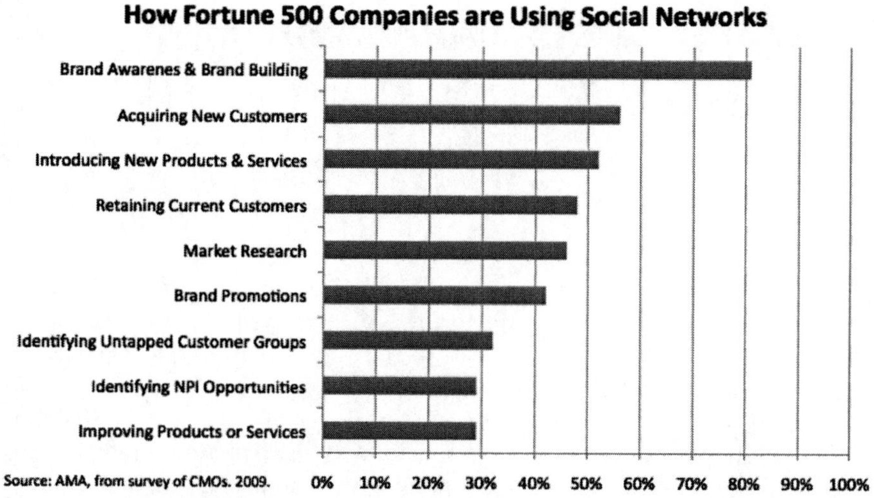

How Fortune 500 Companies are Using Social Networks

Brand Awarenes & Brand Building	
Acquiring New Customers	
Introducing New Products & Services	
Retaining Current Customers	
Market Research	
Brand Promotions	
Identifying Untapped Customer Groups	
Identifying NPI Opportunities	
Improving Products or Services	

Source: AMA, from survey of CMOs. 2009.   0% 10% 20% 30% 40% 50% 60% 70% 80% 90% 100%

Figure 5.7 American Marketing Association survey of Fortune 500 Chief Marketing Officers, 2009, about how their businesses are currently using social networks.

An individual's way of presenting herself or himself in social media channels may have a strong influence on the opportunities to make a good career with the desired employers. First, companies Google potential employees and their social media presence when applying for a job, both for reasons of checking their competence and social profile, and to discover potential problems. Second, a positive presence on Facebook, LinkedIn, Xing or Twitter may generate great contacts which an individual would not get access to through other channels—and of course, the wrong presence may decrease the opportunities of getting the desired contacts. Third, a blog or other similar tool may strengthen an individual's current position and her power. For instance, the CEO of a Swedish investment bank has thousands of individuals following his Twitter on a daily basis. He is twittering Monday through Saturday about different themes related to business and finance, which has made him more popular among customers and colleagues (Lomberg & Dunér, 2011).

The importance of social media is large and increasing which emphasises the reach and scope of the social environmental dimension of a society. Revolutions and grassroots movements in countries like Egypt and Iran operate through social media, and a lot of communication in situations where communication is not allowed to take place—incognito or not— through social network platforms.

6 Generation Y as Consumers and Coworkers

This final chapter discusses the Generation Y cohort on a concrete, individual level, i.e., how all the forces and characteristics of the society, the market environment and the social environment described in earlier chapters translate into values, preferences and behavioural traits of Generation Y individuals.

Not only does this chapter, as the title suggests, deal with Generation Y individuals in their roles as consumers and coworkers. It also discusses the emerging society where roles are getting increasingly overlapping and traditional boundaries between work and leisure time are getting blurred. In the emerging Generation Y society, much of what has been taking for given may be subject to change.

After having read the earlier chapters in this book, the driving forces in the development should be rather clear to the reader. Two themes conclude the development—the strong influence of elements from the consumption sphere, and the presence of market forces in contexts where market forces and commercialism were restricted before. The consumerisation of the labour market has been going on for decades but has really taken off in the last decade or so, starting more or less when Generation Y first entered the labour market.

This book has dealt with how society, the market environment and the social environment influence individuals' values, priorities and consumption patterns in a broad sense, something that is manifested in everyday life when individuals live, socialise, consume, work or have leisure activities. The attitudes towards work, leisure time and self-realisation have changed significantly over time at an aggregate level. For individuals, the likeliness of having a particular set of values and behavioural traits varies with many contextual conditions—geographical, ideological and confessional, financial conditions, and also family structure, if the individual lives in a metro or rural area, and a lot more. This book has emphasised that the generational component in the set of values, preferences and behavioural traits that, taken together, constitute an individual might be significant. In learning to know an individual or a small group of people, the generational component is one among many factors to consider. It must not always be more important than other components but should always be considered when a qualified consumer versus coworker analysis is to be undertaken.

For marketing professionals, the generational component is, in most cases, very significant and its importance beyond any doubt. In approaching markets, marketers try to find the right balance between being specific and try to catch unique characteristics of individual customers on the one hand and approaching all customers in the same way, i.e., not segmenting at all on the other hand. Finding groups or segments of consumers that have strong, homogeneous bonds is at the core of marketing thinking and something that should be considered in trying to find an effective marketing approach (cf. Yankelovich & Meer, 2006; Weinstein, 1994).

Over time, it has become more difficult to segment markets by traditional means. First, consumer behaviour has become more fragmented and more difficult to forecast. As there are more choices in the market, customers are less loyal and companies under pressure from manufacturing overcapacities continuously try to come up with innovations and new features. Hence, customers have many reasons to switch brand or exchange the product for one in another category, which is further emphasised by changed consumer attitudes towards loyalty and switching brands. Moreover, an increasing part of the consumption can now be derived from lifestyle and luxury consumption. A couple of decades ago, most products were bought for reasons of survival or fulfilling everyday needs, and only a limited part of sales was driven by emotional purchase criteria. Over time, the percentage of emotional consumption has increased and buying something one does not need by its very meaning is a more fickle purchase process than buying something one needs for survival or everyday life (basic food ingredients, car fuel, electricity, etc.).

Few organisations have the resources to fully explore segmentation opportunities. So in the balancing act between adapting the message to every potential customer and seeing the whole market as a segment, companies should raise a number of questions:

- *Do we understand the customer purchase process?* If the product and purchase situation at hand is emotional, the purchase process is likely to be spontaneous and difficult to catch and conceptualise (cf. Dunning, 2007). And some customer groups are more emotional than others.
- Which customers can we attract—the traditional foundation of segmentation—and *which customers do we want*? The latter requires a more proactive marketing strategy based on a thorough understanding of trends and forces that may have an impact on the future. To proactively approach the future and build relationships with the desired customer groups requires a good orientation in contemporary marketing communication and how the desired customer group/s live

and act. Where are they working? How do they/want to spend their leisure time? What music do they like? Where do they live? For what reasons are they buying? Which ideologies and movements are they embracing?

- *Do we really understand the segments we want to approach and what makes individuals belonging to these segments spend money?* A significant part of the criticism that has been directed towards segmentation emphasises that companies must move beyond demographic variables (Walker, 2007). It has been proven that demographic segmentation lacks the ability to identify segments with high spending patterns or those who value service and emotional performance (cf. Lawrence & Buttle, 2006). Psychographic segmentation has the advantage of identifying several consumer behavioural phenomena, thus providing a deeper understanding about how consumers think and what leads to a certain purchasing behaviour. Personality, attitudes, interests, lifestyles and values are examples of psychographic constructs. However, to succeed with psychographic segmentation, a thorough understanding of the purchase process and whether one deals with a high-involvement or low-involvement product must be at hand (cf. Bolfing, 1988; Richins & Bloch, 1986; Zaichkowsky, 1985).

- *Do we have the right coworkers?* An organisation that really wants to reach a particular customer segment benefits from knowing it from the inside. By having coworkers that share the values of the brand, and really like the company brand, the workplace is likely to be a better and more attractive place (cf. Barrow & Mosley, 2005; Parment & Dyhre, 2009), particularly in the light of values that are important to Generation Y (Parment, 2009c). Coworkers that are part of the desired target segments provide a number of benefits to the company. First, a better understanding of the segment's values, buying considerations, preferences and purchase process, which are likely to result in a more effective and efficient segmentation. Second, a natural way of communicating with the segment through social networks, etc., which makes it easier to relate to and understand the target segment/s. Third, understanding a segment brings the employer brand and the consumer brand closer to each other, thus giving "cross-selling" benefits. Quality and effectiveness in marketing are likely to improve as will the company's brand overall. Poorly targeted market communication is a big cost to companies, and gives a poor impression of the company and its brand. Many consumers have experiences from being contacted and targeted for, as it seems, strange reasons.

- *Do we understand the complexity of branding and how brands in different spheres link to each other?* In the emerging branded society, roles and images are overlapping and that has a thorough impact on segmentation. A company brand is manifested as consumer and employer brand, respectively, in a common conceptualisation. But also the brand of the place where the company, its office and its manufacturing is located, and the country where it is located, matter and influence the brand image. It has long been known that country of origin influences brand image (Erickson et al., 1994; Peterson & Jolibert, 1995; Roth & Romeo, 1992). Moreover, coworkers that share the values of the brand may live somewhere, and increasingly, companies that need qualified workers may have to move to where they live (Parment & Dyhre, 2009).

In a company's efforts to develop an effective segmentation strategy, it is a challenge to take both the advantages of the traditional benefits of segmentation into consideration, while at the same time using segmentation to reach goals that have become increasingly important in the emerging Generation Y society. The bullet points above illustrate questions that marketers should raise with such a modern approach that also take Generation Y into consideration.

SEGMENTATION—A CRUCIAL PART
OF THE MARKETING STRATEGY

Making segmentation a strategic matter, meaning segmentation is a tool that helps the organisation fulfilling its strategic goals, appears increasingly important considering the intensive competition in today's consumer markets. With a broader perspective, segmentation is a key tool in the company's future oriented marketing that puts understanding the Generation Y cohort at the heart of planning for the future. Questions that any company would raise and that reach beyond segmentation are the following:

- *Which industry are we operating in?* Industry boundaries are changing and getting increasingly blurred. As opposed to several decades ago when industry definitions were rather clear, there are now many products in the market for which there is no clear industry classification. And, due to increased insights on the emotional character of many purchases, the fact that individuals buy products for a mixture of reasons, some of which they may not be aware of, makes it difficult and complex to classify the genuine motives for buying an iPad, a vacation travel to New Zealand, a high performance HiFi system or an Audi A5 convertible.
- *What is our main—it might be one or more—competitive advantage/s* (cf. Barney, 1991; Peteraf, 1993; Porter, 1985)? In competitive environments, knowing the strengths of the company and how they translate into something that is an advantage to the customer is crucial to success. Competitive advantages exist also in labour market, often referred to as Employer Value Propositions (O'Donohue & Wickhma,

2008; Savignano, 2010). In the emerging society these are as important as having competitive advantages in consumer markets.

- *How is our brand perceived among different customer groups?* This question is tightly linked to the organisation's ideas about its future profile. Age and generation are important concepts here. Some products and brands are very popular and maintain high market shares for decades but with an emerging generation, the appeal is lost but unless the company follows the brand perception among different age groups, it is unlikely to understand why the brand is losing its appeal.

- *How are we working with marketing communication?* There are significant changes going on in how companies communicate with its—current and potential—customers, and one of the most important driving forces in this development is the growth of grassroots generated information and knowledge—see the case on www.Glass door.com later. Consumers, particularly younger consumers, are getting tired of company-generated information. Companies have largely lost their authority in presenting themselves to the public—individuals increasingly trust grassroots-generated information. As there is an increasing intensity of messages in the public space, it is becoming increasingly difficult to get consumer attention. However, by working smarter with marketing communication, it is still possible to get consumer attention for a reasonable investment, but that requires a thorough understanding of how marketing communication should be designed to reach the desired audience (Parment & Söderlund, 2010). In general terms, many traditional marketing communication channels—outdoor advertising, radio and television commercials, and magazine ads—have difficulties reaching target groups while more recently conceptualised channels—brand ambassadors, co-branding events, Facebook groups, blogs and product placement, etc.—are worth considering since they may be more effective and efficient.

It is hard to imagine situations when the generational cohort component does not matter. For generic products like butter, ice cream, public transport and newspapers, the generational component is less likely to be of high relevance—it is a pronounced strategy that the product at hand should be available to a broad public. However, marketing communication still might be adjusted to fit the values and preferences of different segments. Here, the generational dimension often appears important. Considering the case of domestic travel, a number of means of transport compete and it is therefore a competitive situation. Most domestic train operators, bus companies, etc., apply a general approach that should satisfy everybody's needs. But many people find this strategy boring and reactive. By applying a target group-specific marketing communication, the company can build a stronger reputation and establish better relationships with each segment.

Those days are gone when consumers were seen as an anonymous mass taking advice from the selling company. Segmentation grew important during the age of mass marketing, when consumers were still seen as a large number of individuals which responded to communication, stimuli and offers undertaken by the company. Interactivity is now something natural for all companies. Today consumers are active and companies have many opportunities to get feedback on consumers' search and purchase patterns through website feedback, loyalty cards, etc. However, a systematic effort to catch feedback does not come naturally, at least not in big international enterprises whose business models were organised based on an assumption of mass marketing and companies in power designing their selling and distribution systems in a way that was good for the enterprise (cf. early distribution theory, e.g., Alderson, 1957; Bowersox, Smykay, & La Londe, 1961, 1968; Bucklin, 1966, 1967).

Now, companies need to take opportunities to get fast customer feedback and stay in contact with how young consumers particularly perceive the company's consumer and employer brands. As there is a steady flow of preferences from younger people to older, and less so the other way round, companies need to consider that in their marketing. Older consumers use consumption as a way to stay and feel young. At the same time, few young individuals apply the consumption and clothing style of older people, just to feel and look old. A number of decades ago, the situation was different and there was a stronger flow from older to younger individuals: At the time, seniority largely meant power and in many professions, younger people imitated older colleagues as a way to learn the codes of conduct. Although this still applies to an extent, it appears clear that society has undergone *a transition from seniority as power source to competence, customer orientation and flexibility as power sources* both in carrying out work and in serving customers.

THE CONSUMERISATION OF THE LABOUR MARKET

At the end of this book, and in its last chapter, it is time to sum up the conclusions that might be drawn based on the analysis undertaken. The main outcome of the development described in this book is that *labour markets are increasingly taking over characteristics of consumer markets*, however, there appears to be no flow in the other direction. This chapter will deal a lot with this development, which provides a great challenge not only for businesses but also for NGOs and others in need of a qualified workforce.

In order to stay in contact with what is happening in the marketplace, every organisation needs a sufficiently diversified workforce where young coworkers—Generation Y and other young cohorts—are a natural part of the continuous effort to vitalise the organisation and keep pace with what is happening in the marketplace. Hence, seeing Generation Y as a natural part of the workforce is something every organisation should do—maybe with a few exceptions such as senior clubs or companies only targeting older customers.

There are two changes, which both have been going on for a long time, that made this new situation come about. First, labour markets, earlier strongly regulated by the state, laws, unions, employer–employee agreements, etc., have become more flexible in structural terms. State deregulation has in some cases been necessary to make the labour market function better when demand patterns fluctuate and companies ask for a flexible workforce. If employing a person implies extensive coworker rights, companies may be reluctant to employ. Hence, if *employee protection earlier was a defining characteristic of a well-working society* with a lot of job safety for individuals, as e.g., in Scandinavia, this has now changed. Today, employing somebody is not likely to be an engagement for a lifetime for any of the involved parties. Neither the employer nor the employee wants that. Companies increasingly present their career opportunities in a way that reflects this transition to a new state of flexible coworkers and flexible employers alike. Interestingly, for Generation Y individuals, the biggest fear may not be to lose the job, but to *lose attractiveness in the job market. The best protection for an individual in the labour market today is to stay attractive.* This insight, which obviously is a provocation for those embracing the old, one-firm commitment principle, is crucial and is manifested in the attitudes of young people:

> I started working after graduating when I was 22, and I have been with the same employer for four years now. This really makes me stressed. I like working here and I like my employer, but I feel my friends' attitudes: 'still at the same place after four years?' (female, 26 years, working for a public organisation in a rural area)

The only way for an individual to make sure she or he is really attractive in the labour market is to apply for a new job. According to surveys with Young Professionals, representing data from several European countries (Universum, 2009), wanting more potential for development, wanting to try something new and trying out how attractive one is in the labour market all rank among the top 10 criteria why we apply for a new job. It appears reasonable to assume that reasons for changing jobs with Generation Y will be even more geared towards finding out whether, and to what extent, one is attractive in the labour market.

There is little doubt that *the transition from loyalty and one-firm commitment as the norm, which guided coworkers and also rewarded them for being loyal, to the new situation where coworkers change jobs to realise themselves* is inspired by the consumption sphere. As we will see later in this chapter (Figures 6.1 through 6.4), the criteria for choosing employer among Generation Y individuals now have little to do with the old wisdom that suggests work is for survival and supplying the family with food and roof.

COMPETITION AND MARKETISATION

Not only has deregulation shaped individuals but also the marketisation that took off starting in the 1980s in most countries, a development that largely was driven by the public sector (cf. New Public Management; Ferlie et al., 1996; Hood, 1995; Schedler, 2006). New technology made open and fast communication possible, which in combination with deregulation made the diffusion of marketisation rather fast. Later, in the 1990s, when the Internet gained penetration and power, it further contributed to making individuals more open to be customers also when using public services, and trying new choices if they were not happy with the services supplied.

It is beyond any reasonable doubt that competition in consumer markets is very intensive in many industries—at least with the criteria we know and use. Older people particularly may find the current situation very challenging compared to the less competitive, more closed markets that existed largely until the 1980s. In the last decade particularly, competition has gone global and international companies and distribution channels have taken over a large part of the market—WalMart, McDonald's, Disney, Nike, Apple, IKEA, Hennes & Mauritz, Toyota, Volkswagen and Starbucks are examples of companies in different industries that have strengthened their competitiveness while local suppliers have lost competitiveness or even perished. As an example of how individual companies perceive and interpret the competitive situation, a decade ago, actors in the automobile industry were seriously bothered by the very intense competition and expressed it thus (interviews carried out in 2002, referred in Parment, 2009a, p. 1):

> It goes towards overcompetition, I can't see it improving, it only gets worse. The whole industry is in a state of flux. (Dealer)

> The industry is out of balance, there is no elasticity, it has become harder, the business in general; I think just basically the whole society is going wrong, and that's a very global thing, I don't think the manufacturer is going wrong, I don't think the dealers are going wrong, it's a combination, what we can deliver, we struggle to deliver the brand, the customers are expecting more for less, the customers are very demanding. (Dealer)

In the first decade of the new millennium, competition intensified in many industries. One indication of the competition is *manufacturer overcapacity*. In the 1990s, the automobile industry suffered from an overcapacity of 30 to 40%, at the end of 2008, it was estimated to be 68%. Similar tendencies exist in many industries: Competition is getting increasingly global, and ownership is getting more international. And, not surprisingly, great coworkers become increasingly important in dealing cleverly with all the demands that are at hand.

MARKET FORCES GUIDE TALENTS TO SELF-REALISATION AT WORK

Since the turn of the century, Talent Management and Employer Branding have been themes extensively dealt with by researchers and practitioners, and there is a great deal of management literature on these themes. The early literature from the first years of the millennium have an approach—reflected in their titles—that may be seen as provoking compared to ideals that have dominated in society for decades—loyalty, one-firm commitment and the state taking care of weaker coworkers in many countries, particularly in Europe. Titles such as *The War for Talent* (Michaels et al., 2001); *Winning the Talent War* (Woodruffe, 1999); *Winning the Talent Wars* (Martin & Tulgan, 2001); *Innovation in Human Resource Management: Tooling Up for the Talent Wars* (Reed, 2001); *Winning the People Wars: Talent and the Battle for Human Capital* (Johnson, 2000) challenged existing conceptions about coworkers. We had certainly known for a long time that coworkers are important, but these books strongly emphasised the need for recruiting the best talents.

The focus on top talents turned out to be exaggerated and unbalanced for many businesses. During the first decade of the new millennium, practitioners—and management book authors—gradually came to realise that *right talent* is a better conception than *best talent*. Hiring and overpaying overqualified individuals who leave the organisation as soon as a new opportunity arises causes more problems than it solves (cf. Parment & Dyhre, 2009).

Regardless of whether the focus is on *right talents* or on *top talents*, market forces have come at the heart of relations in labour markets. There are several reasons for this development. First, individuals changing jobs more often means they are exposed to the labour market's evaluation more often. In applying for a new job, the individual tries to investigate her chances of getting the job, and the company does due diligence to make sure the coworker fulfils the requirements. Second, the transparency created by new technology and a more open attitude (few young people would hesitate to share their wage information and grading of the company they work for with other people) makes it a lot easier to compare offers in labour markets—just like it has been for decades in consumer markets. Third, companies under pressure to be profitable, satisfy customers and fulfill expectations on CSR, great HR policies, etc., need great coworkers to be able to succeed. They are therefore willing to offer something more to a coworker who performs well in relation to the organisation's goals. Fourth, mobility causes further mobility and this process reveals the underlying market forces of individual coworkers and employers alike. When a person applies for, and gets, a new job, her old employer is likely to have a vacancy which means a new person must be appointed which in turn creates further mobility, inside the organisation or in the company that the newly employed leaves. This sounds very static, and obviously, the old principle of *filling positions* on the organisational schedule has gradually and to a varying extent been replaced by an approach where qualified coworkers influence the way work is organised, thus making use of their competencies and giving them opportunity to realise their goals. If there was one controller per country region before, a qualified person may now have two or three regions. If a junior auditor proves very qualified in dealing with clients' tax issues, she or he may not get qualified cases after 1 year in office, while the old wisdom suggested nobody should run his or her own cases until 42 years of age (since that might irritate older colleagues and undermine the not explicitly stated seniority principle). However, in principal terms, there is no doubt increasing mobility in the labour market gives many reasons for organisations to restructure the organisation, appoint new bosses, get rid of or redeploy underperforming coworkers, cancel organisational units, start up new businesses, etc. And the message to those who rely on the benefits of one-firm commitment is clear: There may soon be a new situation, a new boss, a new young coworker, or new, demanding customers so you need to stay competitive as coworker. If not, your future inside and outside the organisation you now work for is not as secure as it used to be.

The effects of the development described previously are clear: The old principles do not apply anymore, and many key labour market concepts—employee safety, employer–employee relationships, coworker flexibility, career planning, etc.—are interpreted differently by Generation Y. The labour market is undergoing a fundamental transition that is strongly linked to the emergence of Generation Y as coworkers. The emergence of Generation Y in the labour market affects supply–demand mechanisms and fundamentally changes characteristics of the labour market. With the perspective introduced in this book, it is thus suggested that the labour market is subject to consumerisation.

Table 6.1 emphasises key differences between the traditional approach and the emerging, Generation Y influenced approach to labour markets. Each of the points made in the table to an extent reflects the consumerisation of the labour market.

Generation Y individuals are increasingly looking at their jobs and careers as a continuous flurry of opportunities to learn and perfect themselves. Having grown up in a branded society overcrowded with commercial messages and a never-ending supply of choices and opportunities, Generation Y individuals thus bring their values, which to a large extent are inspired by the consumption sphere, the popular culture, etc., to work

Table 6.1   Key Differences Between Established Conceptions About the Labour Market and Conceptions That Gain Foothold With the Emergence of Generation Y

	Traditional	*Emerging*
Employee safety	Through one-firm commitment.	Through staying attractive in the labour market, e.g., by changing jobs and working with qualified and demanding clients.
Employer–employee relationships	The employee should be happy to have a job. The employer is in power.	Qualified employees are in power—like attractive workplaces.
Coworker flexibility	Coworkers provided flexibility in terms of working style and work hours.	Coworkers' workload varies, and they try to catch customers' desires.
Career planning	Initiated by the employee, largely hidden to coworkers and the employer.	Open on LinkedIn and in employees' discussions with the employer.
What is rewarded	Hours put in, complying with rules and principles, satisfying customers.	Performance, satisfying customers, contributing to the organisation's profitability.

life, thus changing the attitudes towards the employee–employer relationship and how work is being done. Generation Y see work as a venue of self-realisation and the boundaries between work and leisure time are becoming blurred. Hence, consumer and labour markets converge in some critical dimensions and show similar characteristics when it comes to how coworkers approach work, work–life balance, choose employer (assuming there is a choice) and deal with job offers.

An increase in the number of choices in the marketplace, high availability of cheap goods from low-cost countries, the emergence of the Internet and a relative calm period in international politics characterise the coming-of-age experiences of Generation Yers. The popular culture has influenced their values, attitudes and preferences and made them used to many choices, limited loyalty and high demands on self-realisation. Leisure time—a concept not used very much by the Generation Y cohort—is not about preparing for working hard by getting more energy, but rather worklife is an extension of the individual's attempts to maximise opportunities in life.

Technology has enabled comparisons of offers in the labour market, thus, in combination with Generation Y attitudes, makes it clear that in numerous fundamental respects, the labour market is influenced by and increasingly showing a character that is similar to the consumer market.

LABOUR MARKET IN TRANSITION

This section will present driving forces in the consumerisation of the labour market with focus on characteristics of the labour market.

The labour market increasingly demands *individuals with a broad framework, education and way-of-thinking*, which reflects a situation where a new set of criteria are important in carrying out work effectively and efficiently: A person who is flexible, customer-oriented, varies the hours and effort spent on work, and knows how to present herself and the work tasks in a good and varying way depending on the target group has great chances of performing well in today's labour market.

Regardless of whether the individual is working with product development, quality management, investor relations, manufacturing, machinery maintenance, housing or handling tax issues, a balanced approach with an understanding of how different parts of the organisation contribute to the organisation's shared effort is necessary.

The increased focus of companies on employer branding, recruitment and the application process has largely contributed to individuals being active CV builders at an early stage. This is a global phenomenon, and the more companies work across borders, the more similar recruitment processes will be. Many industries have experienced strong consolidation in terms of ownership, and big international companies have merged and grown, both at the manufacturer level and at the retail level (cf. Parment & Dyhre, 2009), brands have become more global and global brands have gained increased market shares in many markets. Globalisation has thus made employees in different parts of the world more similar to each other.

> Even if the national, political and economic backgrounds of these 'Yers' are very different, it is surprising to see how core similarities can be observed throughout the world, within any graduate population. (De Wazieres, 2008, p. 21)

More flexible working hours applies in many industries. However, some companies report serious problems because of this change, since it is difficult to hold the organisation together if coworkers choose to work at hours that fit their wants. This change is related to the change in the attitude towards the work–leisure time interface discussed in Chapter 1. Particularly in more qualified jobs both coworker attitudes and the nature of the work speak for flexible hours being a phenomenon also in the future.

Pressure on effectiveness, profitability, flexibility and satisfying customers force through new working approaches. For instance, less time is now in many organisations spent in physical meetings. If tradition suggested there should be a meeting every Tuesday morning—and everyone should be there—an emerging approach might be to have a meeting when there is a need to. And if attendance is limited it may depend on the meeting not being necessary.

Shorter working life. We invest more and more time in education but we do not necessarily retire later. During the remaining working years, there is more pressure to perform well and more intensively, and individuals are forced to collect their life income in a shorter time period. As people live longer and expect to have more active years as seniors, they need to earn more money in a shorter time period. Seniors today are likely to need more money than earlier generations as they are used to higher living standards, and are in a better condition which makes travelling, dining out and other costly activities more attractive. According to a number of studies, this "grey market" is expected to grow substantially in the future (cf. Chaston, 2009). There is likely to be a higher degree of flexibility with the working– not working interface in the future, i.e., seniors will even more than today vary their job efforts and the period of partly working may be very extensive—maybe from the age of 60 until 72, 75 or 78.

Another manifestation of the increased transparency and more market forces is the phenomenon of *customers evaluating coworkers*. While earlier, there was less openness in this respect and *voting with the feet* was the likely consequence of customer dissatisfaction, organisations now ask for and customers are willing to give feedback on individual coworkers. The advantage is clear: Customer complaints are clearly addressed to the employee so a situation where a customer leaves without the organisation knowing what happened is less likely. On the other hand, this phenomenon, among many other things treated in this book, makes life tough for low performers.

Individuals are expected to take more responsibility for their careers. A good education at a state university is no longer a guarantee for getting a good job, and the philosophy of state school systems over time has undergone a transition from providing knowledge in core subjects like language training, mathematics, etc., and making people good citizens to helping people finding strategies to develop learning themselves. Earlier, people were provided with knowledge. State and government responsibility and intervention level have changed in many countries, and, at the same time, *unions have shifted their focus* to helping members develop working life based on the changed conditions instead of maintaining the status quo. These changes put increased pressure on people to take responsibility for their own careers and personal development.

THE EVALUATION APPROACH FROM CONSUMER MARKETS NOW IS USED IN LABOUR MARKETS

For some years now, consumer markets have been characterised by intensive competition accompanied by feedback and evaluation systems that make market forces very obvious in how individuals and organisations choose between existing alternatives. More recently, approaches, tools and attitudes from consumer markets have gained foothold also in labour markets.

Box 6.1   Taking the Evaluation Approach from Consumer Markets
to the Labour Market: Glassdoor.com

"What would happen if someone left the unedited employee survey for the whole company on the printer and it got posted to the Web?"

That was the question Glassdoor.com's co-founder Robert Hohman asked his long-time friend Rich Barton, who founded travel site Expedia in 1994. Robert and Rich contemplated why it's so difficult to find helpful information about jobs and workplaces. Robert called on good friend Tim Besse and they expanded the survey concept to include salary details down to the job level and CEO approval ratings. The career and workplace community Glassdoor. com was born in late 2007 to deliver new transparency to the job market.

Glassdoor.com provides an opportunity for anyone to find and anonymously share salary details about specific jobs for specific employers or company and interview reviews describing life on the inside of an employer. All these services are for free. All information comes from the people who know these companies best and, in most cases, have no or little interest in projecting an overwhelmingly positive image of the workplace—either the employees who work there or the candidates who have been interviewed there. Before users get access to all of the information shared by others on Glassdoor.com, they are asked to post an anonymous salary, company review or interview review.

Glassdoor.com is growing rapidly but with main focus on America. In Spring 2009, reviews of 20,000 companies were available. One year more than 84,000 companies were available. Then, the growth of companies slowed down, but that's for a simple reason: Most companies operating in the U.S. of a sufficient size are now on Glassdoor.com. And the amount of data is growing at a fast pace. Glassdoor provides real-time salary/compensation details by title and company, thus answering questions such as the employees' overall grading of a company or how much a Marketing Manager at Booz Allen, Apple, Hennes & Mauritz, Pfizer or Siemens earns a year? Moreover, detailed company reviews give pros and cons based on what employees on the inside really think with reviews and ratings that hit on the good, the bad, and a lot more in between. Interview reviews allow anyone to get information from the inside on a company's interview and hiring process.

Also people in the labour market not currently applying for a job available at any of the companies available at Glassdoor.com are likely to benefit from interview reviews that provide a perspective into the overall experience and difficulty of an interview.

Glassdoor.com reflects a new era in society—that of consumer and coworker power, and transparency. There are certainly methodological problems with the type of websites where users provide all the information—e.g., websites that provide hotel reviews, client-based ranking of hospitals and student-based university rankings. Despite that, websites like Glassdoor.com are very important and reflect a transition of the job market from a market with employers in power to one where employees may have the upper hand.

References: www.Glassdoor.com, accessed May 2009 through February 2011; Parment & Dyhre (2009) *Sustainable Employer Branding*, Per J Håkansson speech at Universum Awards 2009, *Building Online Employer Brands Using Social Media Tools*, March 23rd in Stockholm and May 19th in Berlin.

One example of tools that are inspired by evaluation platforms in consumer markets is the web site www.Glassdoor.com. It emphasises how technological changes, in this case a web based user evaluation platform, fundamentally change the preconditions for communication and exchanging information in the marketplace. Potential employees now can get information on a potential employer on the Internet, and the quantity and quality of this information is likely to improve day by day.

PERSONAL CHARACTERISTICS THAT BENEFIT FROM THE DEVELOPMENT

With a new generation, one may find that somebody who enjoyed attention and attractivity before does not really fit with the values and preferences the new generation portrays. There are personal characteristics and behavioural traits that have almost guaranteed success in the past, but have now largely lost their relevance, and there are other characteristics and traits that once were not really appreciated. Being able to present oneself in a clever way on different Internet platforms, e.g., LinkedIn, and knowing how to deal with integrity issues—what to say, where and when are other factors that have always been important but even more so today: Mistakes are now more evident, diffuse more rapidly and may be stored.

Individuals possessing great social skills, and a high ability to be flexible with the level of engagement and care are likely to benefit from the development described in this book. The same holds for being unshy and taking opportunities that arise, even if it means moving to a new place or giving up some benefits. When people change jobs more often, they are likely to lose some benefits since every employer has a unique coworker benefit schedule.

All in all, *market forces* will get stronger and *constraining factors*, e.g., company policies, renumeration systems that give people benefits for what they did in the past, etc., will lose power. In an increasingly competitive and transparent environment, organisations including public organisations, will not have resources to pay people for something they did in the past so performance measurement and reward systems are likely to be less focused on past performance. Measuring and rewarding performance is something that should be carefully considered and there are is lot of literature on how to balance the short and long term, individual and group focus, etc. (cf. Merchant & Van der Stede, 2007; Nilsson et al., 2011, Olve, & Parment, 2010).

CRITICAL EMPLOYEES VITALISE THE ORGANISATION AND MAKES IT MORE FIT AND COMPETITIVE

As was discussed in Chapter 2, Generation Y individuals are not being as stressed by (unanswered) e-mails as their older colleagues who are used to answering every incoming inquiry or question addressed to him or her. Generation Y's more critical attitude towards the multitude of inquiries and requests that come from many sources inside and outside the organisation may be a benefit for the organisation. Generation Y has developed some skills in knowing which e-mails, requests and questions are important and should be taken time with, and those that may rather be seen as opportunities and options which must not be considered.

Every organisation has a zone of activities that is initiated and implemented without a clear management idea or customer benefit behind. These activities, which are very limited in some organisations with tight top management control and heavy pressure on efficiency but vast in other instances, reduce organisational effectiveness and competitiveness. Every industry and organisation has been subject to an increased number of demands over time, which often results in questions and inquiries from external stakeholders, and interorganisational initiatives and processes that tax on the organisation's resources. A new workforce generation that is skeptical against the effort required to deal with all this may, at the end of the day, be good for the organisation, its working climate, its attractivity as employer, and the profitability.

As one Generation Y individual puts it: "Having grown up with all these choices and vast information about everything, the introductory university lecture on critical thinking was a joke. As a small guy I learned to select and value information. You don't need a university degree to do that."

Examples of too uncritical older colleagues and the waste of organisational resources are numerous. Here are a few examples, which are all collected during the research projects presented in this book, with older coworkers who apply a way-of-thinking that applied a few decades ago, when there were fewer choices and less demanding stakeholders.

- A big church with more than 2,000 members has severe problems derived from a heavy imbalance between income, which is lower than it used to be, and a too large administration combined with too many activities. When asked to reduce the extensive travel (5 to 7 weeks a year) that senior pastors engage in, they say "What would people say? We have been to these conferences and events for decades. They would be disappointed we wouldn't show up". Afraid of losing members and visitors, activities which attract very few people are kept running. Obviously, a lack of ability to close down activities results in a reactive attitude that is likely to reduce the church's attractiveness and ability to get tithes from members and visitors.
- A leading university issued an award for the best course plan of the year, and two senior lecturers won. They said they spent more than 100 hours writing it—too much for a rather standardised document of two pages. Most lecturers spend a few hours on writing a course plan, or even less. Organisations should not reward

individuals for overallocating resources to activities of limited strategic importance.

- A leading car manufacturer has won several prizes for the best instructor's manual of the year. Inspired by this, this activity is maintained and developed. However, more than 90% of Generation Y individuals say they don't use instructor's manuals. "If there is a need to, the product is not constructed in a good way. I would buy another product for which I don't need a manual to find out how it works", says a typical Generation Y statement. Obviously, the car manufacturer spends a lot of money and resources on an activity that is losing interest among customers—and not only Generation Y is reluctant to read instructor's manuals. Even worse, those who engage in these activities are getting credits, attention and prizes which may make the organisation less willing to develop and take in what is going on among key customer groups and young consumers particularly.

- A bachelor student at a leading university with 30,000 students was disappointed by the fact that he only had the opportunity to present his bachelor thesis two times a year. He wanted to do it when it fit his study and career plan. Not considering the opportunity to finish the thesis and then wait until the next opportunity to present it arises, he wrote an e-mail to the University vice-chancellor, whose administrative staff set up a number of meetings with key personnel and then, finally, a meeting with the student, the Director of Studies, the Dean of the Business School, and the Head of the Faculty of Social Science. Why should a Rector, his office and a Dean engage in this? Obviously, the student did not have a serious complaint about something that worked improperly or could have been a danger to the university's reputation. There are few or no universities where students can take courses and examine exactly when students want to.

- A leading auditing firm spends a lot of effort on Employer Branding, and they are doing it in a systematic and thought-through way. Students appear to like the approach and the auditing firm is highly ranked among students, who know the Employer Branding activities but haven't met the organisation's main body of coworkers yet. A few older partners, with a great influence on the organisation's values, priorities and culture, expressed very old-fashioned values which would embarrass most young coworkers. Jokes such as "so you are working part-time?" when people leave the office at 7:30 p.m. are inappropriate and effectively contribute to forcing Generation Y and other Young Professionals to look for another job. In partner-owned organisations, the attitudes of older colleagues are particularly important, since they are owning the business and decide which young coworkers will get the opportunity to develop their careers and finally become partners. Too little knowledge about Generation Y will make it very difficult for this auditing firm to recruit and keep the best talents for the purpose of developing the organisation's competitive abilities.

- A service organisation in a competitive environment is afraid of getting a competitive disadvantage, so it tries to consider every client and stakeholder request and demand, and also competitive moves. However, this has resulted in supporting functions expanding and, as a consequence, the organisation is close to getting a competitive disadvantage based on its inability to run the core business. An organisation must know why it exists and what its top priorities are. Being focused on customers does not mean every demand should be met. Maybe something could be learnt from Ryan Air, a company that does little or nothing by the book but it has a clear focus—efficient core business and low prices. And it has proven successful in an industry with competitors being afraid of getting competitive disadvantages.

FROM AGE AND YEAR-IN-OFFICE TO PERFORMANCE

Society has always rested on *the seniority principle*, an assumption that suggests that age and year-in-office are linked to respect, authority, influence over others and a comparatively high level of rewards. With this perspective, executives of high age had more influence on decisions than their younger colleagues. Grandfather and grandmother had a say over the parents in raising the children. Recruitment policies rested on the policy of year-in-office: Many politicians, sales managers and head of schools were recruited based on their experiences and insights collected during a life course in the same organisation. As employer loyalty was high, particularly for senior employees, a high age normally meant many years in office.

Things are changing, though. Air carrier Scandinavian Airlines System, known for being subject to strong influence from unions, finally broke the seniority principle when they made an agreement with the union in 2004 to recruit air pursers based on competence and suitability—until then, the year-in-office principle was the sole criteria. Ever since, a 35-year-old steward/ess may have 60-year-old subordinates: However, it was first after Swedish Worker's Right Court decided that air pursers should be chosen based on skills, not primarily on seniority, that this change took place (cf. judge AD 2006:89 in the Swedish Worker's Court).

The year-in-office principle remains an important criteria in organising work, particularly in industries with a high level of income per employee and a tradition of rewarding one-firm commitment. Lawyer and auditing firms have benefited from the privilege of selecting among the best students from the best universities, and then apply an "up or out policy", meaning that peer competition determines who will stay and who will have to leave. Typically, after 15 to 20 years, a limited percentage of those who started their careers in the company get the opportunity to become partners.

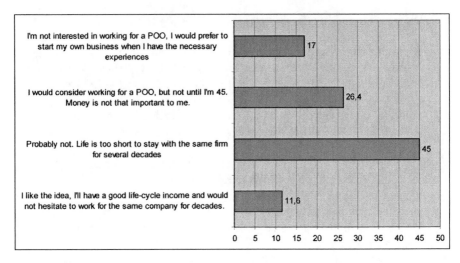

Figure 6.1   Eighty eight percent of the Generation Y cohort hesitate to work for a partner-owned organisation (POO), e.g., a lawyer or accounting firm.

From a life-cycle income perspective, the business and career model of partner organisations makes sense. Employees who are finally promoted by existing partners to become partners have a high lifetime income and the tough competition among peers makes sure the organisation provides a high level of competence and motivation in dealing with qualified assignments for their clients.

However, in the light of Generation Y values and traits, the model is likely to lose attractiveness and power. When the desired coworkers want to change jobs a few times in their first 10 career years, it will be more difficult to keep them. If earlier the employer in most cases decided which people to keep and which had to look for another job, this power has gradually moved to the coworkers who have the information, technology, attitudes and courage to change jobs if they find that doing so makes sense.

A reasonable effect of this change, which is difficult to measure, is that the profile and qualities of people that are recruited deteriorates. Assuming a lawyer or auditing firm got many applicants representing the 15th best percentile of graduates in the past, when the company's business and remuneration model was in line with what the applicants wanted, they may now get applicants from a lower percentile. If the company does not notice this change, the attitudes towards younger coworkers may worsen. In addition to existing problems of older coworkers seeing younger colleagues as inexperienced and less qualified (which, to a certain extent, is true)—and these may be significant in partner-owned organisations with vast differences in income, status and freedom at work in comparing coworkers of different age—a new problem is added. "Back in the early 1980s, when I started working here, we were way smarter and more qualified than the young guys coming in now"—such attitudes, which are sometimes expressed by coworkers in their 50s and 60s, portray coworker values and effectively hinder young coworkers from feeling welcome. And, as there are many other nice places to work for qualified people, such attitudes effectively inform young people that they should start working for another organisation where their competences and characteristics are appreciated.

CRITERIA FOR CHOOSING JOB IN A CONSUMERISED LABOUR MARKET

The changes and the emerging situation that this book is trying to understand and explain are manifested in the attitudes Generation Y express in describing their ideal employer. There are several companies running surveys on ideal employers, e.g., Universum. For major, well-known companies rankings of ideal employers may give a lot of information about how the organisation's attractiveness develops. However, smaller organisations may not be considered and not all companies are listed in the surveys (companies pay a fee to get listed). For any type of organisation it is a great challenge to package, repackage, present and communicate the organisation's offer to potential employees. In this process, considering what Generation Y individuals find interesting in choosing employer—assuming there is a choice—should be important.

The survey referred to in Figures 6.1 through 6.4 has been run at a selection of universities in the U.S., Canada, Brazil, Sweden and New Zealand among social science and management students belonging to Generation Y (more on this in the methodological considerations enclosure). Each of the criteria in Figures 6.1 through 6.4 is derived from interviews with Generation Y individuals and research on this cohort. The results mirror the findings that are presented in this book. For instance, one dimension that is important to Generation Y is the location of the workplace. This is not just about everyday logistics and access to public transport, something earlier generations found crucial in choosing workplace, but also about how they want to live their lives. In city centers, which are places that Generation Y individuals in general appreciate, there is great access to services of different kinds, to shopping and to after work activities with friends, alumni friends and members of different social networks the individual belongs to. When companies move out of the city center to save money through lower office rent, they at the same time run the risk of losing attractiveness among Generation Y individuals who want to make use of everything a city center, but hardly a suburb, offers. A Generation Y individual with 450 Facebook friends and an intensive activity with former colleagues through LinkedIn is trying to build her personal brand by promoting herself in different contexts. Lunches are an important venue for this purpose, and a city center

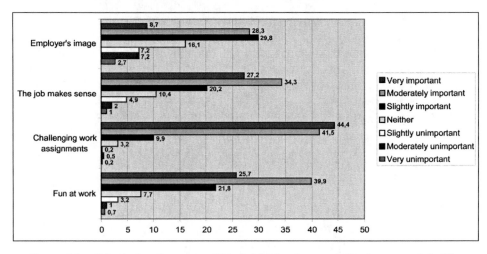

Figure 6.2   Criteria for Generation Y individuals when applying for a new job (Figures 6.2 through 6.4), based on a methodology which assumes that the individual has a choice of place to work. The categories are derived from in-depth interviews with Generation Y individuals. Source: Multinational Employer Branding Survey (2010).

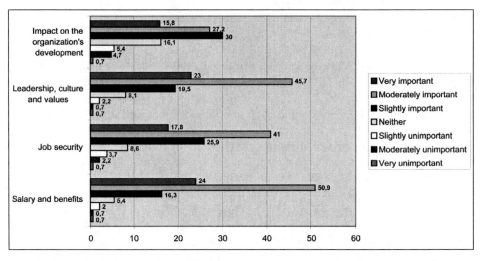

Figure 6.3   Criteria for Generation Y individuals when applying for a new job. Source: Multinational Employer Branding Survey (2010).

with maybe hundreds of attractive lunch restaurants has a strong advantage over an industrial park.

Generation Y individuals prefer the workplace to be located not too far from home. Accordingly, it is easier to attract talented employees if the workplace is located in an area where many qualified coworkers live.

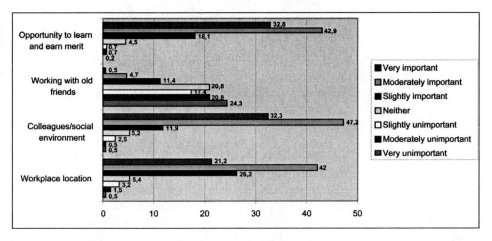

Figure 6.4 Criteria for Generation Y individuals when applying for a new job.
Source: Multinational Employer Branding Survey (2010).

Business travel is not something that brings prestige to the individual who is travelling if the individual belongs to Generation Y. A Lufthansa Gold Membership status, something that brought prestige to a busy person in the past, is now indicating that the individual has to fly to her clients instead of the other way round.

All in all, the criteria that Generation Y represent in choosing employer reflect a new, emerging society where individual career plans, self-realisation and having fun or a nice time whenever it is possible are put at the center of Generation Y's life strategies.

TO CONCLUDE . . .

This book rests on the assumption that first when a new generation has incorporated all the characteristics of an emerging society will its full effects be understood.

This book is not a political book that is trying to promote young people or put forward everything that is a problem with them: It is a book on understanding generational cohorts, with the main focus on Generation Y, and how they function in consumer and labour markets, both at an aggregate and at an individual level. The four levels dealt with—society and the values that characterises society; the market environment; the social environment; and the individual—taken together have constituted a framework for understanding Generation Y. To understand a generation, it is crucial to, as has been suggested, consider the coming-of-age experiences, i.e., the years between 17 and 23 of age particularly, in forming an individuals values and preferences.

Throughout the book has explored Generation Y and their role as consumers and coworkers in an emerging postmodernist society, which one needs to understand to be able to compare and contrast Generation Y with earlier generations. Having grown up in a branded society overcrowded with commercial messages and a never-ending supply of choices and opportunities, Generation Y not only influences consumption patterns, they have also brought their values to work life, thus changing attitudes towards career, the employee–employer relationship and how work is being done. Generation Y particularly sees work as a venue of self-realisation which is manifested in the emotional and self-realisation focused criteria of an ideal employer. The boundaries between work and leisure time have become blurred—thus the consumer and labour markets converge in some critical dimensions. And that is also the message of the book: The labour market is subject to consumerisation as a consequence of Generation Y applying a consumption sphere influenced approach onto work.

METHODOLOGICAL CONSIDERATIONS

The structure of the empirical data is described in the Preface of this book. The 35 interviews have been collected based on the following methodological considerations. The interviews were based on an interactivity between the researcher/s and the participant/s where both parts perform their stories, negotiate their identities, and construct meaning through interpersonal processes (Holstein & Gubrium, 1995). Particularly at the beginning of the empirical data collection, there was a considerable openness for new, emerging ideas and themes proposed by the interviewee. The interview situation may be seen as a collaborative, communicative event where social interactions are structured by researchers and interviewees (cf. Hammersley & Atkinson, 1996). Social reality and how reality is discussed during the course of an interview are intertwined, with interviews mediated through language and jointly accomplished through the exchanged acts of hearing and telling a story (Holstein & Gubrium, 1995). The interviews were carried out in English, German and Swedish, languages of which the interviewer, i.e., Anders Parment, has good knowledge about. However, as Swedish is the mother tongue and English and German second languages, some nuances related to lack of an in-depth understanding of the language spoken may have arisen. On the other hand, the knowledge the study aims at collecting is not extremely sensitive to language nuances.

Insights from anthropology suggest that one's position within or outside the defined boundary of an experience will impact the interview process and outcome. Moreover, an anthropologist standpoint suggests that where the researcher enters the research site as an insider—which is measured in terms of e.g., race, gender or class—the tacit knowledge that the familiarity with the group represents results in a different outcome. The knowledge is likely to be different to that available to the outsider (cf. McGinn, 2005; Tashakkori & Teddlie, 2003).

The survey referred to in Figures 6.2 through 6.4 has been run at a selection of universities in the U.S., Canada, Brazil, Sweden and New Zealand among social science and management students born between 1980 and 1990. There are different ways of putting the data together. For instance, based on this set of questions, some minor differences between HR students and business students have been found, however, they are not significant and will not change the overall results of the findings, which represent the tendency in the Generation Y cohort to appreciate employer criteria that are emotional, contribute to self-realisation and an individual's well-being.

Notes

NOTES TO THE PREFACE

1. Former French president François Mitterand quoted in De Wazieres (2008).
2. Socrates quoted in e.g., Ayers, W., & Ladson-Billings, G. (2001). *To teach: The journey of a teacher.* Teacher's College Press.
3. Pollack, L. (2010, October 26). How millennial women are shaping our future. *The Huffington Post.*

NOTES TO CHAPTER 1

1. Woolwridge (2006).
2. Pink (2002) quoted in Parment & Dyhre (2009).
3. On-site visit at Kone in Chicago, June 2007.

NOTES TO CHAPTER 2

1. Björkman, A. (2009). Disaster investigation; The German 'Group of Experts' (2006). Investigation report on the capsising on 28 September 1994 in the Baltic Sea of the Ro-Ro Passenger Vessel MV Estonia.
2. cf. Helsen et al. (1993), Mahajan et al. (1990) on diffusion patterns in marketing.

NOTES TO CHAPTER 3

1. All quotes in this section from *Vogue*, British Edition, July 2010, unless otherwise stated.
2. There are an increasing number of male models that started their careers as actors, however this case focuses on female modelling.
3. More on this theme might be read in Savage, J. (2008). *Teenage. The creation of youth 1875–1945.* Pimlico; and Fowler, D. (2008). *Youth culture in modern Britain, c. 1920–c.1970.* Palgrave Macmillan.

NOTES TO CHAPTER 5

1. Socrates quoted in, e.g., Ayers, W., & Ladson-Billings, G. (2001). *To teach: The journey of a teacher.* Teacher's College Press.

Bibliography

Aaker, D.A. (1991). *Managing Brand Equity. Capitalizing on the Value of a Brand Name,* New York: The Free Press.

Aaker, D. (2010). *Building strong brands.* UK: Simon & Schuster.

Achterholt, G. (1988). *Corporate Identity. In zehn Arbeitsschritten die eigene Identität finden und umsetzen,* Wiesbaden: Gabler.

Ahmad, A. (2011). Social Network Sites and Its Popularity. *International Journal of Research and Reviews in Computer Science,* 2(2), 522–526.

Akass, K., & McCabe, J. (Eds.). (2004). *Reading Sex and the City.* London: I. B. Tauris & Co.

Åkerberg, A. (1998). *Meanings of Relationships in Knowledge-Intensive Work Contexts,* Doctoral Dissertation No. 70, Swedish School of Economics and Business Administration, Helsingfors.

Alavi, M., & Leidner, D. E. (2001). Review: Knowledge management and knowledge management systems: Conceptual foundations and research issues. *MIS Quarterly,* 25(1), 107–136.

Alden, D. L., Steenkamp, J.-B. E. M., & Batra, R. (1999). Brand positioning through advertising in Asia, North America, and Europe: The role of global consumer culture." *Journal of Marketing,* 63, 75–87.

Alderson, W. (1957). *Marketing behaviour and executive action. A functionalistic approach to marketing theory.* Homewood, IL: Irwin Inc.

Arnold, D. (1992). *The Handbook of Brand Management,* London: The Economist Books.

Asthana, A. (2004, June 6). Star babies push buggy battles to new heights. *The Observer.*

Ayers, W., & Ladson-Billings, G. (2001). *To Teach. The Journey of a Teacher.* Second edition, New York: Teachers College Press.

Bakewell, C., & Mitchell, V.-W. (2003). Generation Y female consumer decision-making style. *International Journal of Retail and Distribution Management,* 31(2), 95–106.

Banerjee, S. B., Lyer, E. S., & Kashyap, R. K. (2003). Corporate environmentalism: Antecedents and influence of industry type. *Journal of Marketing,* 67(2), 106–122.

Barak, B., & Schiffman, L. G. (1981). Cognitive age: A nonchronological age variable. In K. B. Monroe (Ed.), *Advances in consumer research,* 8, 602–606. Ann Arbor, MI: Association for Consumer Research.

Barksdale, H. C., & Darden, W. R. (1972). Consumer attitudes towards marketing and consumerism. *Journal of Marketing,* 28–35.

Barney, J. (1991). Firm resources and sustained competitive advantage. *Journal of Management,* 17, 99–120.

Barrow, S. & Mosley, R. (2005). *The Employer brand. Bringing the Best of Brand Management to People at Work*, West Sussex: Wiley & Sons.

Batra, R., Ramaswamy, V., Alden, D. L., Steenkamp, J.-B. E. M., & Ramachander, S. (2000). Effects of brand local and nonlocal origin on consumer attitudes in developing countries. Journal of Consumer Psychology, 9(2), 83–95.

Battaglio, S. (2010). *Who are TV's top earners?* Retrieved February 1, 2011 from www.tvguide.com

Bergqvist, E. (2009). *Du är din generation [You are your generation]*, Stockholm: Norstedts.

Bell, M. L., & Emory, C. W. (1971). The faltering marketing concept. *Journal of Marketing, 35,* 37–42.

Bienkowski, W., Brada, J., & Radlo, M.-J. (Eds.). (2006). *Reaganomics goes global. What can the EU, Russia and transition countries learn from the USA?* New York, N.Y.: Palgrave Macmillan.

Birkigt, K., Stadler, M. M., & Funck, H. J. (1992). *Corporate identity, Grundlagen, Funktionen, Fallbeispiele.* Landsberg/Lech: Verlag Moderne Industrie.

Bolfing, C. P. (1988). Integrating consumer involvement and product perceptions with market segmentation and positioning strategies. *Journal of Consumer Marketing, 5*(2), 49–57.

Bowersox, D., Smykay, E., & La Londe, B. (1968). *Physical distribution management. Logistics problems of the firm.* New York/London: MacMillan.

Bowersox, D. J., Smykay, E. W., & La Londe, B. J. (1961). *Physical distribution management. Logistics problems of the firm.* New York: The Macmillan Company.

Brod, C. (1984). *Technostress: The human cost of the computer revolution.* Reading, MA: Addison-Wesley.

Brunnström, L. (Ed.). (2004). *Svensk industridesign: En 1900-talshistoria, 2: a upplagan,* Stockholm: Prisma.

Brunsdon, S. (2008). *Feminist television criticism, second edition.* Oxford: Open University Press.

Bryant, N. (2010). *Oprah impresses Sydney during Australia visit.* BBC News, Entertainment & Arts, December 14.

Bucklin, L. P. (1966). *A theory of distribution channel structure.* Cambridge, Massachussets: IBER Special Publications.

Bucklin, L. P. (1967). Postponement, speculation and structure of distribution channels. In B. Mallen (Ed.), *The Marketing Channel: A conceptual viewpoint* (pp. 67–74). New York: Wiley.

Buddensieg, T., Rogge, H., & Yhyte, B. (1985). Industrielkultur. Peter Behrens and the AEG, 1907–1914. *Design Issues, 2*(1), 90–93.

Bulbeck, P. (2010, December 14). Wraps 'Ultimate Australian Adventure'. *The Hollywood Reporter.*

Bush, V. (1945, July). As we may think. *Atlantic Monthly,* 47–61.

Buskirk, R. H., & Rothe, J. (1970). Consumerism—An interpretation. *Journal of Marketing, 34,* 61–65.

Carswell, A., Byrnes, H., & Fife-Yeomans, J. (2010, December 14). Oprah slams funding criticism for her Australian trip. *Herald Sun [Australia].*

Castrogiovanni, G., & Justis, R. (1998). Franchising configurations and transitions. *Journal of Consumer Marketing, 15*(2), 170–190.

Chalmers, D., Davies, G., & Monti, G. (2010). *European Union Law. Second edition,* Cambridge: Cambridge University Press.

Chaston, I. (2009). *Boomer marketing.* Oxon/London: Routledge.

Chester, E. (2002). *Employing Generation Why? Understanding, managing, and motivating your new workforce.* Vacaville, CA: Chess Press.

Clement, D. (2008, February 2). Why businesses need Generation Y. *Weekend Herald,* F7.

Cockrell, K., Cockrell, D., & Harris, E. L. (1998). Generational variability in the understanding and use of technology. *Alberta Journal of Educational Research*, 44(1), 111–114.

Coughlan, A., Andersson, E., Stern, L., & El-Ansary, A. (2001). *Marketing channels* (6th ed.). Upper Saddle River, NJ: Prentice Hall.

Cutler, S. J. (1977). Aging and voluntary association participation. *Journal of Gerontology*, 32, 470–479.

Davenport, T. H., De Long, D. W., & Beers, M. C. (1998). Successful knowledge management projects. *Sloan Management Review, Winter*, 43–57.

Davies, J. R. (2010). *The European consumer citizen: A coherent, tangible and relevant notion of citizenship?* Doctoral dissertation, University of Leicester.

Demartini, J. R. (1985). Change agents and generational relationships: A reevaluation of Mannheim's problem of generations. *Social Forces*, 64(1), 1–16.

Deshpande, R. (1983). 'Paradigms Lost': On theory and method in research in marketing. *Journal of Marketing*, 47, 101–110.

De Wazieres, F. (2008). Millennials in the workplace . . . for the best. *Universum Quarterly*, No. 2, 20–21.

Dick, A. S., & Basu, K. (1994). Customer loyalty: Toward an integrated conceptual framework. *Journal of the Academy of Marketing Science*, 22(2), 99–113.

Dou, W., Want, G., & Zhou, N. (2006). Generational and Regional Differences in Media Consumption Patterns of Chinese Generation X Consumers. *Journal of Advertising*, 35(2), 101–110.

Duncan, T. & Moriarty, S.E. (1997). *Driving Brand Value: Using Integrated Marketing to Drive Stakeholder Relationships*, New York: McGraw-Hill.

Dunning, D. (2007). Self-Image Motives and Consumer Behavior: How Sacrosanct Self-Beliefs Sway Preferences in the Marketplace. *Journal of Consumer Psychology*, 17(4), 237–249.

Dutton, J. E., Dukerich, J. M., & Harquail, C. V. (1994). Organisational images and member identification. *Administrative Science Quarterly*, 39(2), 239–263.

Ecclestone, K., Biesta, G., & Hughes, M. (2009). *Transitions and learning through the lifecourse*. London: Routledge.

Egharevba, I. (2001). Researching an-'other' minority ethnic community: Reflections of a black female researcher on the intersections of race, gender and other power positions on the research process. *International Journal of Social Research Methodology*, 4, 225–241.

Eisenstadt, S. N. (1956). *From generation to generation*. Glencoe, IL: Free Press.

Elder, Glen H., Jr. (2008). Time, human agency, and social change: Perspectives on the life course. *Social Psychology Quarterly*, 57(1), 4–15.

Elster, J. (1983). *Sour grapes: Studies in the subversion of rationality*. Cambridge, UK: Cambridge University Press.

Erickson, G. M., Johansson, J. K., & Chao, P. (1984). Image variables in multiattribute product evaluations: Country-of-origin effects. *Journal of Consumer Research*, 11, 694–699.

Evans, M., Jamal, A., & Foxall, G. (2006). *Consumer behaviour*. Chicester: John Wiley & Sons.

Featherstone, M., & Hepworth, M. (1991). The mask of ageing and the postmodern life course. In M. Featherstone & B. Turner (Eds.), *The body, social processes and cultural theory* (pp. 371–389). London, UK: Sage.

Fenner, R., Paton, J., & Saminather, N. (2010, December 22). Oprah stars in Australia's $3 million tourist drive. *Bloomberg Business Week*.

Ferlie, E., Ashburner, L., Fitzgerald, L., & Pettigrew, A. (1996). *The new public management in action*. Oxford: Oxford University Press.

Freeman, M. A., & Bordia, P. (2001). Assessing alternative models of individualism and collectivism: A confirmatory factor analysis, *European Journal of Personality*, 15(2), 105–121.

Fry, C. & Keith, J. (1982). The Life Course as a Cultural Unit. In Riley, M.W. & Teitelbaum, M.S., *Aging from Birth to Death*, Boulder: Westview Press, 51–70.

Fuller, S. (2001). *Knowledge management foundations*. Oxford: Butterworth Heineman.

Garfield, B. (2007, March 26). The post advertising age. Bob Garfield's chaos scenario 2.0. *Advertising Age*, 1–10.

Gerstner, R., & Hunke, G. (2006). *55 plus marketing. Zukunftsmarkt Senioren*. Wiesbaden: Gabler.

Gigerenzer, G. & Goldstein, D.G. (1996). Reasoning the Fast and Frugal Way: Models of Bounded Rationality. *Psychological Review*, 4, 650–669.

Gigerenzer, G., & Selten, R. (2002). *Bounded rationality: The adaptive toolbox*. Cambridge, Massachusetts: MIT Press.

Gilleard, C., & Higgs, P. (2002). The third age: Class, cohort or generation? *Ageing and Society*, No. 22, 369–382.

Goldsmith, M., Ulrich, D., & Rampersad, H. K. (2009). *Authentic personal branding: A new blueprint for building and aligning a powerful leadership brand*. Greenwich: Information Age Publishing.

Gravett, L., & Throckmorton, R. (2007). *Bridging the generation gap. How to get radio babies, boomers, Gen Zers, and Gen Yers to work together and achieve more*. New Jersey: Career Press.

Green, B. (2003). *Marketing to leading-edge baby boomers, perceptions, principles, practices, predictions*. Ithaca, NY: Paramount Market Publishing Inc.

Grein, A. F., Craig, C. S., & Takada, H. (2001). Integration and responsiveness: Marketing strategies of Japanese and European automobile manufacturers. *International Journal of Marketing*, 9(2), 19–50.

Grenier, A.M. (2007). Crossing Age and Generational Boundaries: Exploring Intergenerational Research Encounters. *Journal of Social Issues*, 63(4), 713–727.

Gubrium, J. & Sankar, A. (Eds.), *Qualitative Methods in Aging Reearch*, Newbury Park, CA: Sage.

Haigh, D., & Knowles, J. (2004). How to define your brand and determine its value. *Marketing Management*, 3(3), 22–28.

Hammersley, M., & Atkinson, P. (1996). *Ethnography: Principles in practice*. New York: Tavistock.

Haugland, S. A. (2010). The integration-responsiveness framework and subsidiary management: A commentary. *Journal of Business Research*, 63(1), 94–96.

Helleloid, D., & Simonin, B. (1994). Organisational learning and a firm's core competence. In Hamel G. & Henne A. (Eds.), *Competence-based competition*. Chichester: Wiley.

Helsen, K., Jedidi, K., & DeSarbo, W. S. (1993). A new approach to country segmentation utilizing multinational diffusion patterns. *Journal of Marketing*, 57, 60–71.

Herbig, K., Koehler, W., & Day, K. (1993). Marketing to the baby bust generation. *Journal of Consumer Marketing*, 10(1), 4–9.

Higgs, P. F., Myde, H., Gilleard, C. J., Victor, C. R. ,Wiggins, R. D., & Jones, I. R. (2009). From passive to active consumers? Later life consumption in the UK from 1968–2005. *Sociological Review*, 57, 102–124.

Hill, R. (1970). *Family development in three generations*. Cambridge, MA: Schenkman Publishing Co.

Himma, K. E. (2007). The concept of information overload: A preliminary step in understanding the nature of a harmful information-related condition. *Ethics and Information Technology*, 9, 259–272.

Holbrook, M.B. & Schindler, R.M. (1989). Some Exploratory Findings on the Development of Musical Tastes," *Journal of Consumer Research, 16*, 119–124.

Holbrook, M.B. & Schindler, R.M. (1994). Age, Sex, and Attitude Toward the Past as Predictors of Consumers' Aesthetic Tastes for Cultural Products. *Journal of Marketing Research, 31*(3), 412–422.

Hollander, S. C. (1960). The wheel of retailing. *Journal of Marketing, 24*(July), 37–42.

Holmes, J. H., & Crocker, K. E. (1987). Predispositions and the comparative effectiveness of rational, emotional and discrepant appeals for both high involvement and low involvement products. *Journal of the Academy of Marketing Science, 15*(1), 27–35.

Holstein, J. A., & Gubrium, J. F. (1995). *The active interview*. Thousand Oaks, CA: SAGE.

Holt, D. B. (2004). *How brands become icons: The principles of cultural branding*. Cambridge, Massachusetts: Harvard University Press.

Hood, C. (1995). The 'New Public Management' in the 1980s: Variations on a theme. *Accounting, Organisation and Society, 20*(2/3), 93–109.

Hopkinson, C. (2005, August 25). It's the end of the road for the celebrity buggy that conquered Britain. Children's Health. *The Telegraph*.

Huntley, R. (2006). *The world according to Y. Inside the new adult generation*. Crows Nest, NSW: Allen & Unwin.

Hung, K.H., Gu, F.F. & Yim, C.K. (2007). "A social institution approach to identifying generataion cohorts in China with a comparison with American consumers. *Journal of International Business Studies, 38*, 836–853.

Giele, J. Z., & Elder, G. H., Jr. (Eds.). (1998). *Methods of life course research: Qualitative and quantitative approaches*. Thousand Oaks, CA: Sage Publications.

Jeacle, I. (2007). Management accounting for consumerism. In T. Hopper, R. Scapens, & D. Northcott (Eds.), *Issues in management accounting* (pp. 27–44). Harlow: Prentice Hall.

Jenkins, S. (2006). *Thatcher & sons: A revolution in three acts*. London: Allen Lane.

Jensen, J. M., & Hansen, T. (2008). An empirical examination of brand loyalty. *Journal of Product & Brand Management, 15*(7), 442–449.

Johnson, M. (2000). *Winning the people wars: Talent and the battle for human capital*. Harlow: Prentice Hall.

Kadatz, H. J. (1977). *Peter Behrens—Architekt, Maler, Grafiker und Formgestalter 1868–1940*. Leipzig: E.A. Seemann.

Kangun, N., Cox, K. K., Higginbotham, J., & Burton, J. (1975). Consumerism and marketing management. *Journal of Marketing, 39*(2), 3–10.

Kapferer, J-N (1997). *Strategic Brand Management. Creating and Sustaining Brand Equity Long Term*, second edition, London: Kogan Page.

Kapferer, J.-N. (2008). *The new strategic brand management: Creating and sustaining brand equity long term*. London: Kogan Page.

Kertzer, D. I. (1982). Generation and age in cross-cultural perspective. In M. W. Riley, R. P. Abeles, & M. S. Teitelbaum (Eds.), *Aging from birth to death* (pp. 15–46). Washinton, D.C.: Westview Press for American Association for the Advancement of Science.

Kertzer, D. I. (1983). Generation as a sociological problem. *Annual Review of Sociology, 9*, 125–149.

Kotler, P. (1972). What consumerism means for marketers. *Harvard Business Review, 50*(May–June), 48–57.

Kotler, P., Armstrong, G. & Parment, A. (2011). *Principles of Marketing*. Swedish edition, Harlow: PrenticeHall.

Lawrence A. & Buttle, F. (2006). Customer retention management processes: A quantitative study. *European Journal of Marketing, 40*(1/2), 83–99.

Lawton, M.P. & Herzog, A.R. (Eds.) (1989). *Special Research Methods for Gerontology*, Amityville, NY: Baywood Publishing Co.

Levitt, T. (1960). Marketing Myopia. *Harvard Business Review, 38*(4), 45–56.

Lipkin, L.A. & Perrymore, A.J. (2009). *Y in the Workplace, Managing the 'Me First' Generation*, Career Pr. Inc.

Littrell, M. A., Yoon, J. M., & Halepete, J. (2005). Generation X, baby boomers, and swing: Marketing fair trade apparel. *Journal of Fashion Marketing and Management, 9*(4), 407–419.

Lomberg, S., & Dunér, H. (2011, January 29). Så kan din nätprofil ge karriärskjuts, *E24*. Retrieved 2011–02–05 from www.e24.se

Lusch, R. F., Vargo, S. L., & O'Brien, M. (2007). Competing through service: Insights from service-dominant logic. *Journal of Retailing, 83*(1), 5–18.

Lyttkens, L. (1988). *Politikens klichéer och människans ansikte*, Stockholm: Akademeja.

Lyttkens, L. (1991). Uppbrottet från lagom. En essä om hur Sverige motvilligt tar sig in i framtiden. Stockholm: Akademeja.

Maglin, N. B., & Perry, D. (1996). Bad girls. In *Good girls: Women, sex and power in the nineties*. New Brunswick: Rutgers University Press.

Mahajan, M., Muller, E., & Bass, F. M. (1990). New product diffusion models in marketing: A review and directions for research. *Journal of Marketing, 54*, 1–26.

Mannheim, K. (1952/1927). The problem of generations. In P. Kecskemeti (Ed.), *Essays on the sociology of knowledge* (pp. 276–320). New York: Oxford University Press.

Mannheim, K. (1956). *Essays on the sociology of culture*. New York: Oxford University Press.

Markert, J. (2004). Demographics of age: Generational and cohort confusion. *Journal of Current Issues and Research in Advertising, 2*(2), 11–25.

Martin, C. A., & Tulgan, B. (2001). *Managing Generation Y*. Amerherst: HRD Press.

McAllister, J. & Harris, A.L. (2003). *GenXegesis: Essays on Alternative Youth (Sub)culture*, Madison: University of Wisconsin Press/Popular Press.

McGinn, M. K. (2005). Ethical and friendly researchers, but not insiders: A response to Blodgett, Boyer, and Turk. *Forum Qualitative Sozialforschung/Forum: Qualitative Social Research, 6*(6), Article 37.

Merchant, K. A. & Van der Stede, W.A. (2007). *Management Control Systems: Performance Measurement, Evaluation, and Incentives,* London: Prentice Hall.

Meredith, G., & Schewe, C. (1994). The power of cohorts. *American Demographics, 16*(12), 22–31.

Meredith, G. E., Schewe, C. D., Hiam, A., & Karlovich, J. (2002). *Managing by defining moments: America's 7 generational cohorts, their workplace values, and why managers should care.* New York: Hungry Minds.

Meredith, G. E., Schewe, C. D., & Karlovich, J. (2002). *Defining markets, defining moments: America's 7 generational cohorts, their shared experiences, and why businesses should care.* New York: Hungry Minds.

Michaels, E., Handfield-Jones, H. & Axelrod, B. (2001). *The War for Talent.* Harvard: Harvard Business Press.

Moncrief, W. C., Babakus, E., Cravens, D. W., & Johnston, M. W. (2000). Examining gender differences in field sales organisations. *Journal of Business Research, 49*(3), 245–257.

Morris, M. (2001). Contradictions of post-modern consumerism and resistance. *Studies in Political Economy, 63*(Spring), 7–32.

Nilsson, F., Olve, N.-G., & Parment, A. (2011). *Controlling for competitiveness.* Liber: Copenhagen Business School Press.

Niskanen, W. A. (1988). *Reaganomics: An insider's account of the policies and the people.* Oxford: Oxford University Press.

Nonaka, I., & Takeuchi, H. (1995). *The knowledge-creating company. How Japanese companies create the dynamics of innovation.* New York: Oxford University Press.

Oakley, A. (1981). Interviewing women: A contradiction in terms. In H. Roberts (Ed.), *Doing feminist research* (pp. 30–62). London: Routledge & Kegan Paul.

O'Donnell, M. (1995). *Age and generation, society now.* Social science paperbacks, No. 301, London: Taylor and Francis.

O'Donohue, W., & Wickhma, M. (2008). Managing the psychological contract in competitive labour-market conditions. *Journal of Global Business Issues, 2*(2), 23–31.

Öhgren, A., & Sandkuhl, K. (2008). Information overload in industrial enterprises—Results of an empirical investigation. In R. Dyerson & G. Harindranath, *Proceedings of the 2ⁿᵈ European Conference on Information Management and Evaluation* (pp. 343–350). University of London, Reading: Academic Publishing Limited.

Olins, W. (1989). *Corporate Identity. Making business strategy visible through design,* London: Thames and Hudson.

Oliver, R. L. (1999). Whence consumer loyalty? *Journal of Marketing, 63*(Special Issue), 33–44.

Overholt, A. (2003). In the hot seat—who: Ginni Rometty. *Fast Company,* Jan. p. 46.

Park, H.-J., Rabolt, N. J., & Jeon, K. S. (2008). Purchasing global luxury brands among young Korean consumers. *Journal of Fashion Marketing and Management, 12*(2), 244–259.

Parment, A., & Dyhre, A. (2009). *Sustainable employer branding—Guidelines, worktools and best practices.* Liber: Samfundslitteratur.

Parment, A. (2007a). Generation Y som konsumenter—en studie av 80-talisters attityder till marknadskommunikation och köpbeteende [Generation Y as consumers—a study into the consumer behaviour and market communication]. *International School of Management and Industrial Engineering, Research Report 2007:3,* Linköping University.

Parment, A. (2007b). Generation Y som medarbetare—en studie av 80-talisters inställning till arbetsgivare, arbete och karriär" [Generation Y as coworkers—their attitudes towards career and work life]. *International School of Management and Industrial Engineering, Research Report 2007:4,* Linköping University.

Parment, A. (2008a). Distribution strategies for volume and premium brands in highly competitive consumer markets. *Journal of Retailing and Consumer Services, 15*(4), 250–265.

Parment, A. (2008b). En underverderet forandringskraft, *Ungdomsforskning,* No. 3, October, 21–30.

Parment, A. (2008c). *Generation Y—Framtidens konsumenter och medarbetare för entré (The emergence of Generation Y as consumers and co-workers).* Liber.

Parment, A. (2008d). *Marknadsför till 55 plus (Baby boomer marketing).* Liber.

Parment, A. (2009a). *Automobile marketing. Distribution strategies for competitiveness.* Saarbrücken: VDM Verlag.

Parment, A. (2009b). Erwartungen der Generation Y an den Arbeitgeber. *Oscar Trends,* No. 1, 47–55.

Parment, A. (2009c). *Generation Y—Mitarbeiter der Zukunft. Herausforderung und Erfolgsfaktor für das Personalmanagement.* Gabler.

Parment, A. (2011). *The global integration and local adaptation dilemma: Does it apply to premium brands?* EIRASS 18th International Conference on Recent advances in Retailing and Services Science, San Diego.

Parment, A. & Söderlund, M. (2010). *Det här måste du också veta om marknadsföring,* Malmö: Liber.

Parry, D. C. (2005). Women's experiences with infertility: The fluidity of conceptualizations of 'family'. *Qualitative Sociology, 28*(3), 275–291.

Peteraf, M. A. (1993). The cornerstones of competitive advantage: A resource-based view. *Strategic Management Journal, 4*(3), 179–191.

Peterson, R. A., & Jolibert, A. J. P. (1995). A meta-analysis of country-of-origin effects. *Journal of International Business Studies, 26*, 883–900.

Phoenix, A. (1994). Practising feminist research: The intersection of gender and "race" in the research process. In M. Maynard & J. Purvis (Eds.), *Researching women's lives from a feminist perspective* (pp. 49–71). London, UK: Taylor and Francis.

Pollack, L. (2010) *How Millennial Women are Shaping Our Future*, Oct. 26th, Retreived from www.huffingtonpost.com on Dec. 10th, 2010.

Porter, M. (1985). *Competitive advantage. Creating and sustaining superior performance.* New York: The Free Press.

Pratten, C. F. (1987). Mrs. Thatcher's economic legacy. In K. Minogue & M. Biddiss (Eds.), *Thatcherism: Personality and politics* (pp. 72–94). Basingstoke: Macmillan.

Purkiss, J., & Royston-Lee, D. (2009). *Brand you: Turn your unique talents into a winning formula.* London: Artesian Publishing LLP.

Purvis, J. (2004). Grrrls and women together in the third wave: Embracing the challenges of intergenerational feminism(s). *NSWA Journal, 16*(3), 93–123.

Reed, A. (2001). *Innovation in human resource management: Tooling up for the talent wars.* Wimbledon: Chartered Institute of Personnel and Development.

Reichert, T., & Lambiase, J. (Eds.). (2005). *Sex in consumer culture: The erotic content of media and marketing.* Mahwah, NJ: Lawrence Erlbaum Associates Inc.

Reinartz, W., & Kumar, V. (2002). The mismanagement of customer loyalty. *Harvard Business Review*, s. 4–12.

Rentz, J. O., Reynolds, F. D., & Stout, R. G. (1983). Analyzing changing consumption patterns with cohort analysis. *Journal of Marketing Research*, February, 12–20.

Richins, M. L., & Bloch, P. H. (1986). After the new wears off: The temporal context of product involvement. *The Journal of Consumer Research, 13*(2), 280–285.

Roberts, J. A., & Manolis, C. (2000). Baby boomers and busters: An exploratory investigation of attitudes toward marketing, advertising and consumerism. *Journal of Consumer Marketing, 17*(6), 481–497.

Rogler, L. H. (2002). Historical generations and psychology: The case of the Great Depression and World War II. *The American Psychologist, 57*(12), 1013–1023.

Rogler, L. H., & Cooney, R. S. (1984). *Puerto Rican families in New York City: Intergenerational processes.* Maplewood, NJ: Waterfront Press.

Roth, K., & Morrison, A. J. (1990). An empirical analysis of the integration-responsiveness framework in global industries. *Journal of International Business Studies, 21*, 541–564.

Roth, M. S., & Romeo, J. B. (1992). Matching product category and country image perceptions: A framework for managing country-of-origin effects. *Journal of International Business Studies, 23*, 477–497.

Rotschild, M. L. (1979). Advertising strategies for high and low involvement situations. In J. Maloney & B. Silverman, *Attitude research plays for high stakes* (pp. 74–93). Chicago: American Marketing Association.

Ryder, N.B. (1965) The Cohort as a Concept in the Study of Social Change. *American Sociological Review, 30*(6), 843–861.

Salzer, M. (1994). *Identity across borders—A study of the IKEA world.* Doctoral dissertation, Department of Management and Economics, Linköping University.

Savignano, M. (2010). Multiple identities of an employer: A case study on DHL. Munich: GRIN Verlag.

Scandura, T. A., & Williams, E. A. (2000). Research methodology in management: Current practices, trends, and implications for future research. *Academy of Management Journal*, 43(6), 1248–1264.

Scanorama. (2011). SAS Fleet. No. 6, 112.

Schedler, K., & Proeller, I. (1996). *New public management*. 3. *Auflage*, Haupt Berne Verlag.

Schewe, C., Carlsson, B., & Parment, A. (2011). *History matters: Understanding Swedish generational cohort segments and capturing their minds, hearts and consumption power.* Sent for journal review.

Schewe, C., & Meredith, G. (2004). Segmenting global markets by generational cohorts: Determining motivations by age. *Journal of Consumer Behaviour*, No. 4, 51–63.

Schewe, C., & Noble, S. M. (2000). Market segmentation by cohorts: The value and validity of cohorts in America and abroad. *Journal of Marketing Management*, 16, 129–142.

Schindler, R.M. & Holbrook, M.B. (1993). Critical Periods in the Development of Men's and Women's Tastes in Personal Appearance. *Psychology and Marketing*, 10(6), 549–564.

Schimmack, U., Oishi, S., & Diener, E. (2005). Individualism: A valid and important dimension of cultural differences between nations. *Personality and Social Psychology Review*, 9(1), 17–31.

Schuman, H. & Scott, J. (1989). Generations and Collective Memories. *American Sociological Review*, 54, 359–381.

Shank, J. K., & Rauwerdink, W. J. (1974). Midwest Ice Cream Co. *Harvard Business Review*.

Siguaw, J. A., & Honeycutt, E. D., Jr. (1995). An examination of gender differences in selling behaviors and job attitudes. *Industrial Marketing Management*, 24(1), 45–52.

Simon, H. A. (1945). *Administrative behavior: A study of decision-making process in administrative organisation*. New York: The Free Press.

Simon, H. A. (1956). Rational choice and the structure of the environment. *Psychological Review*, 62, 129–138.

Simon, H. A. (1982). *Models of bounded rationality*. Cambridge, MA: MIT Press.

Simon, H. A. (1990). Invariants of human behavior. *Annual Review of Psychology*, 41, 1–19.

Skidelsky, R. (Ed.). (1988). *Thatcherism*. London: Chatto & Windus.

Söderqvist, M. (Ed.) (2010). *80-talisterna – så funkar de. Den kompletta guiden till generationen som stämplar in när 40-talisterna loggar ut [People born in the 1980s – how they are. The complete guide to the generation that clocks in when those born in the 1940s log out]*, Stockholm: United Minds.

Southgate, P. (1994). *Total Branding by Design. How to Make Your Brand's Packaging More Effective*, London: Kogan Page.

Spender, J-C (1996). "Making Knowledge the Basis of a Dynamic Theory of the Firm. *Strategic Management Journal*, 17(Winter Special Issue), 45–62.

Spender, J. D., & Grevesen, W. (1999). The multinational enterprise as a loosely coupled system: The global integration–local responsiveness dilemma. *Managerial Finance*, 25(2), s. 63–84.

Spillane, M. (2008). *Branding yourself: How to look, sound and behave your way to success*. London: Sidgwick & Jackson.

Stanworth, J. (1991). Franchising and the franchise relationship. In. Stanworth, J. & Stanworth, C., *Work 2000: The Future for Industry, Employment and Society* (pp. 175–199). London: Pual Chapman.

Starrin, B. & Svensson, P-G. (Eds.) (1994). *Kvalitativ metod och vetenskapsteori*, Lund: Studentlitteratur.

Stephenson, P.R. & House, R.G. (1971). A Perspective on Franchising. *Business Horizons, 14*(4), 35–42.

Stern, L. (1969). *Distribution Channels: Behavioural Dimensions*, Boston: Houghton Mifflin.

Stern, L.W. & Reve, T. (1980). "Distribution Channels as Political Economies: A Framework for Comparative Analysis. *Journal of Marketing, 44*(Summer), 52–64.

Stern, L.W. (1967). The Concept of Channel Control. *Journal of Retailing, 53*, 14–20.

Stern/MMA (Media-Markt-Analysten) (2001). *Study on Purchase Patterns in the Car Industry*, Frankfurt.

Stinchombe, A.L. (1965). Social structure and organisation. In March, J.G. (ed), *Handbook of Organisations* (pp. 142–193). Skokie, IL: Rand McNally.

Stjerna, M. (2000). Går luften ur internetköpet? *Teknikens Värld, 6*, 56–59.

Sutcliffe, K.M. & Weber, K. (2003). The High Cost of Accurate Knowledge. *Harvard Business Review*, May, 74–82.

Swärd, L. (1998). Privatimport och Internet utmanar Volvochef. *Svenska Dagbladet*, Jan 3.

Swedish Competition Authority (2004). Swedish Competition Authority sues eight car dealers for SEK 157.5 million. *Press release*, March 16.

Szita, J. (2007, June). Work: The next generation. Jobs as we know them are disappearing. That's not necessarily a bad thing. *Holland Herald*, 26–29.

Tacet, D. & Zénoni, G. (1986). *Renault, secret d'Etat*, Paris: Albin Michel.

Tamames, R. (1994). *Introducción a la economía española*, Madrid: Alianza Editorial.

Tashakkori, A., & Teddlie, C. (Eds.). (2003). *Handbook of mixed methods in social & behavioral research*. Thousand Oaks: Sage Publications.

Teece, D. (1996). Firm Organisation, Industrial Structure and Technological Innovation. *Journal of Economic Behavior and Organisations, 31*, 193–224.

Thomas, R. (1993). The valuation of brands. *The Journal of the European Society for Opinion and Marketing Research*, E.S.O.M.A.R, *21*(2), 80–90.

Thomke, S. & von Hippel, E. (2002). "Customers as Innovators. A New Way to Create Value. *Harvard Business Review*, Apr., 74–81.

Thompson, D.N. (1971). *Franchise Operations and Antitrust*, Massechussets: Lexington.

Thorngate, W. (1988). On paying attention. In W. Baker, L. P. Mos, H. V. Rappard, & H. J. Stam (Eds.), *Recent trends in theoretical psychology: Proceedings of the Second Biannual Conference of the International Society for Theoretical Psychology* (pp. 247–264). Berlin: Springer Verlag.

Triandis, H. C. (1993). Collectivism and individualism as cultural syndromes. *Cross-Cultural Research, 27*(3–4), 155–180.

Tsoraklidis, L. (2002). Towards a new motor vehicle block exemption—Commission Proposal for motor vehicle distribution, adopted on 5 February 2002. *EC Competition Policy Newsletter, European Commission*, Bruxelles, *2*(June), 31–34.

Tulgan, B. (2009). *Not everyone gets a trophy: How to manage Generation Y*. Chicester: Jossey-Bass.

Uggla, H. (2003). *Organisation av varumärken: för kapitalisering och affärsutveckling*, Malmö: Liber Ekonomi.

Ulrich, J. M. (2003). Generation X. A sub(cultural) genealogy. In J. M. Ulrich & A. L. Harris (Eds.), *GenXegesis: Essays on alternative youth (sub)culture* (pp. 184–195). Popular Press 3.

Universum (2009). *Ideal Employer Rankings and Young Professionals Surveys*, Stockholm: Universum.

Urrutia, C. (2004). Nueves negocios: Los concesionarios crean un mercado paralelo de piezas. *el mundo motor,* Dec. 23.

van Bruggen, G.H. & Kacker, M. (1998). Sharing Information in Marketing Channels. *Marketing Management: Strategy and Organisation,* 27th EMAC Conference Stockholm 20th–23rd May 1998.

Vargo, S. L., & Lusch, R. F (2004a). Evolving to a new dominant logic for marketing. *Journal of Marketing,* 68(January), 1–17.

Vargo, S. L., & Lusch, R. F. (2004b). The four service marketing myths. *Journal of Service Research,* 6(4), 324–335.

Vaughn, C.L. (1974). *Franchising. Its Nature, Scope, Advantages, and Development,* Massachusetts: Lexington Books.

Vickers, A., Bavister, S. & Smith, J. (2008). *Personal Impact: What it Takes to Make a Difference,* Harlow: Prentice Hall Life.

Vinen, R. (2009). *Thatcher's Britain: The politics and social upheaval of the 1980s.* London: Simon & Schuster.

Vogue. (2010, July). Ageless style: The history of the supermodel. 20 years of power and beauty. British Edition.

Volks, F. & Michaely, P. (2002). Böses im Bilde. *Auto Motor & Sport,* 1, 140–143.

von Seitz, H. (1995). Konvergenz: Theoretische Aspekte und empirische Befunde für westedeutsche Regionen. *Konjunkturpolitik,* 41, Jahrg. H. 2, 168–198.

The Wall Street Journal. (2010, September 14). Oprah Winfrey to film episodes of her show at Sydney Opera House.

Walters, D. & Laffy, D. (1996). *Managing Retail Productivity and Profitability,* Hampshire: MacMillan Business.

Webber, I.E. (1997). *The Automotive Industry.* Final Minority Report, Industry Commission.

Weber, M. (1947). The Theory of Social and Economic Organisation. New York: Free Press.

Weernink, W.O. & Auer, G. (2002). Analysis: Pischetsreider has to move fast to survive at VW. *Automotive News Europe,* Nov. 4.

Weinstein, A. (1994). *Market segmentation.* Chicago: Probus Publication Co.

Welch, D., Roberts, D., Matlack. C., Bush, J. & Romley, I. 2008, Automakers' Overcapacity Problem. *Business Week,* Dec. 31th.

Wernle, B. (2002). Carmakers see a service nightmare. *Automotive News Europe,* Sep. 23.

Westhead, P., Howorth, C. & Cowling, M. (2002). Ownership and management issues in first generation and multi-generation family firms. *Entrepreneurship & Regional Development,* 14, 247–269.

Westrup, K. (2001). Schöner wohnen. *Auto Motor & Sport,* 9, 82–83.

White, J. M., & Klein, D. M. (2007). *Family theories. 3rd edition. London:* Sage Publications.

White Riley, M. (1982). Aging and social change. In White Riley, M., Abeles, R.P. & Teitelabum, M.S., *Aging from birth to death.* Boulder: Westview Press.

Wieland, B. (1996). *Auto Motor & Sport,* various editions.

Wigmore, B. (2008, November 4). Sexually charged shows such as Sex And The City and Friends to blame for rise in teenage pregnancy. *Mail Online.* Retrieved December 2010 from www.dailymail.co.uk

Wileman, A. & Jary, M. (1997). Retail Power Plays. From *Trading to Brand Leadership,* London: MacMillan Business.

Wilson, J. S., & Blumenthal, I. (2008). *Managing brand you. Seven steps to creating your most successful self.* New York: American Management Association.

Wikström, S. & Normann, R. (1994). *Knowledge and Value,* London: Routledge.

Williams, G., Henderson, J., Scheffer, F. & Tongue, A. (1998). *In the Changing Face of Car Distribution.* Case Studies, Research Paper 9/98, July, Chadwick: International Car Distribution Programme Ltd.

Williams, K., Haslam, C., Johal, S. & Williams, J. (1994). *Cars: Analysis, History, Cases,* Rhode Island: Berghahn Books, Inc.

Williamson, Oliver E. (1985). *The Economic Institutions of Capitalism: Firms, Markets, Relational Contracting.* New York.

Wittreich, W.J. (1962). Misunderstanding the Retailer. *Harvard Business Review,* Vol. 40, May-June.

Wohl, R. (1979). *The Generation of 1914.* Cambridge, Massachusetts: Harvard University Press.

Womack, J.P., Jones, D.T. & Roos, D. (1990). *The Machine that Changed the World,* New York: Maxwell MacMillan International.

Wood, E. M. (1991). *The pristine culture of capitalism: A historical essay on old regimes and modern states.* London: Verso.

Woodruffe, C. (1999). *Winning the Talent War: A Strategic Approach to Attracting, Developing and Retaining the Best People,* Oxford: John Wiley & Sons.

Woolridge, A. (2006, October 5). The battle for brainpower. *The Economist,* 1–2.

Wright, C. (2001). As market share falls, Opel must get rid of dealers. *Automotive News Europe,* Jan. 28.

Wright, C., 2002a, Saab to cut ist dealer network in half. *Automotive News Europe,* June 3.

Wright, C., 2002b, VW plans gradual reduction of dealers. *Automotive News Europe,* Jan. 14.

Yankelovich, D., & Meer, D. (2006). Rediscovering market segmentation. *Harvard Business Review,* 84(2), 122–131.

Yin, R.K. (1994). *Case Study Research. Design and Methods.* London: Sage.

Zaichkowsky, J. L. (1985). Measuring the involvement construct. *Journal of Consumer Research,* 12, 341–352.

Zald, M.N. (1970). Political Economy: A Framework for Comparative Analysis. in Alds, M.N., (Ed.), *Power in Organisations,* Nashville, TN: Vanderbilt University Press.

Zentes, J. (1991). Informationssysteme im Marketing. Marketing. ZFP, No. 3, 191–195.

Zettelmeyer, F. (2000). Expanding to the Internet: Pricing and Communications Strategies When Firms Compete on Multiple Channels. *Journal of Marketing Research,* 27, 292–308.

Zhou, L. & Hui, M.K. (2003). Symbolic Value of Foreign Products in the People's Republic of China. *Journal of International Marketing,* 11(2), 36–58.

Zupko, J. (2007). Career decisions depend on personal connection. *Universum Quarterly,* Issue 1, 17.

Index